BURT FRANKLIN: RESEARCH & SOURCE WORKS SERIES 567
Selected Essays in History, Economics & Social Science 183

APPEAL
OF
ONE HALF THE HUMAN RACE
WOMEN
AGAINST
THE PRETENSIONS OF THE OTHER HALF
MEN

"One thing is pretty clear, that all those individuals whose interests are indisputably included in those of other individuals may be struck off from political rights without inconvenience. In this light may be viewed all children up to a certain age, whose interests are involved in those of their parents. In this light also women may be regarded, the interest of almost all of whom is involved either in that of their fathers, or in that of their husbands."—*Encyclopædia Britannica: Supplement: Article on 'Government,'* page 500.

"'Tis all stern duty on the female side;
On man's, mere sensual gust and surly pride."

APPEAL

OF

ONE HALF THE HUMAN RACE

WOMEN

AGAINST

THE PRETENSIONS OF THE OTHER HALF

MEN

TO RETAIN THEM IN POLITICAL, AND THENCE
IN CIVIL AND DOMESTIC, SLAVERY

IN REPLY TO A PARAGRAPH OF MR. MILL'S CELE-
BRATED "ARTICLE ON GOVERNMENT."

By WILLIAM THOMPSON

BURT FRANKLIN
NEW YORK

Published by LENOX HILL Pub. & Dist. Co. (Burt Franklin)
235 East 44th St., New York, N.Y. 10017
Originally Published: 1825
Reprinted: 1970
Printed in the U.S.A.

S.B.N.: 8337-35152
Library of Congress Card Catalog No.: 71-134450
Burt Franklin: Research and Source Works Series 567
Selected Essays in History, Economics and Social Science 183

INTRODUCTORY LETTER

TO

MRS WHEELER.

TOPICS OF LETTER.

Object of Letter: to acknowledge to whom the sentiments of the succeeding pages belong . . . . *page* vi

Anathema against half the human race noticed, because put forward by a friend of general liberty and an advocate of the doctrine of Utility viii

A new state of society—that of " Mutual Co-operation in large numbers," in which interest and duty are made to coincide—is necessary to give equal happiness to both sexes ix

The utility of man's superior strength to the general happiness is balanced by the utility of the peculiar faculty of women in bearing and nurturing infants x

But under " Individual Competition" strength carries every thing: individual competition admits of no compensation for women's peculiar faculties and privations xi

Two circumstances—inferiority of strength, and loss of time in gestation—must render the average exertions of women less available than those of men xi

The more inexcusable and base is the imposition by men of factitious restraints on women in addition to those of nature, and the greater the necessity for their removal xi

Under Individual Competition, even an equality of rights would not give women an equality of happiness with men . . . xi

The pleasures that men now obtain from women are limited, by their exclusions, to those of mere sensual appetite and of domination xii

Though an equality of political rights, followed as it necessarily would be by an equality of civil and domestic rights, would not raise women to an equal command of the means of happiness with men, it would afford them the utmost chances of happiness which the present arrangements of society under the system of individual competition would permit, and would be the only alleviation of its evils . . xiii

The progress of Social Science, superseding the mere pursuit of wealth, the confined object of Political Economy, and substituting the pursuit of happiness, will lead to the " Mutual Co-operation of men and women in large numbers," which can alone produce a real equality of happiness between the sexes, raising both equally in the scale of wisdom, virtue, and enjoyments xiv

INTRODUCTORY LETTER

TO

MRS. WHEELER.

HONORED with your acquaintance, ambitious of your friendship, I have endeavoured to arrange the expression of those feelings, sentiments, and reasonings, which have emanated from your mind. In the following pages you will find discussed on paper, what you have so often discussed in conversation—a branch of that high and important subject of morals and legislation, the condition of women, of one half the human race, in what is called civilised society. Though not to me is that " diviner inspiration given," which can clothe with the grace and eloquence of your unpremeditated effusions the calm stream of argument; though, not having been in the situation you have been, to suffer from the inequalities of sexual laws, I cannot join with a sensibility equal to yours, in your lofty indignation and contempt of the puerilities and hypocrisy with which men seek to cover or to palliate their life-consuming and mind- and joy-eradicating oppressions, tempered always however with benevolence even to the foolish oppressors themselves; though I do not *feel* like you —thanks to the chance of having been born a man—looking lonely on the moral desolation around; though I am free from personal interest in the consideration of this question; yet can I not be inaccessible to the plain facts and reason of the case. Though long accustomed to reflect on this subject, to you am I indebted for those bolder and more comprehensive views which perhaps can only be elicited by concentration of the mind on one darling though terrific theme. To separate your thoughts from mine were now to me impossible, so amalgamated are they with my own: to the public this is indifferent; but to me how flattering, could I hope that any suggestions of mine had so amalgamated themselves in your mind!

The days of dedication and patronage are gone by. It is *not* with the view of obtaining the support of your name or your influence to the cause of truth and humanity that these lines are addressed to you. Truth must stand on its own foundation. The smiles of wealth, of power, or of beauty, are extraneous considerations, and should not be put into the scale to supply the want of argument. Whatever bias of judgement is given to the solicitations of either of these, is so much given to passion or sinister interest, to the prejudice of truth. She is strong, immortal: fear not; she must ultimately, on even ground, prevail.

I address you then simply to perform towards you a debt of justice; to show myself possessed of that sincerity which I profess to admire. I love not literary any more than any other species of piracy: I wish to give every thing to its right owner. Anxious that you should take up the cause of your proscribed sex, and state to the world in writing, in your own name, what you have so often and so well stated in conversation, and under feigned names in such of the periodical publications of the day as would tolerate such a theme, I long hesitated to arrange our common ideas, even upon a branch of the subject like the present. Anxious that the hand of a woman should have the honor of raising from the dust that neglected banner which a woman's hand nearly thirty years ago unfolded boldly, in face of the prejudices of thousands of years, and for which a woman's heart bled, and her life was all but the sacrifice—I hesitated to write. Were courage the quality wanting, you would have shown, what every day's experience proves, that women have more fortitude in endurance than men. Were comprehensiveness of mind, above the narrow views which too often marred Mary Wolstonecroft's pages and narrowed their usefulness, the quality wanting,—above the timidity and impotence of conclusion accompanying the gentle eloquence of Mary Hays, addressed, about the same time that Mary Wolstonecroft wrote, in the shape of an *"Appeal"* to the then closed ears of unreasoning men; yours was the eye which no prejudice obscured, open to the rays of truth from whatever quarter they might emanate. But leisure and resolution to undertake the drudgery of the task were wanting. A few only therefore of the following pages are the exclusive produce of your mind and pen, and written with your own hand. The remainder are our joint property, I being your interpreter and the scribe of your sentiments.

Too many years has remained uncontradicted the anathema of a school of modern philosophy against the claim to the equal use and enjoyment of their faculties of half the human race. In the ponderous though enlightened volumes of the Supplement of the Encyclopædia Britannica; this dastardly anathema might have remained concealed from all eyes but those of the philosophers themselves, had not some patriotic men, overlooking perhaps the interests of women in their zeal for those of men, or not weighing the tendency of the paragraph, extracted the "Article on Government," with others, from the volume where its malignity towards half the human race slumbered, and re-printed it for gratuitous circulation; and had not the author of the "Article" expressly refused to omit or modify the offensive antisocial paragraph respecting women, though requested to do so by one whose lightest suggestion on such a subject ought to have been a command, as his wisdom and benevolence surpass those of the disciples surrounding him, the faculties of many of whom seem calculated to gloat upon the least amiable features only of his philosophy.

Had such a paragraph as that in the title-page been put forward by any of the vulgar hirelings or every-day bigots of existing institutions, it would have appeared to you and to me too worthless, from its palpable and audacious falsehood, to merit a reply. But put forward under the shield of philosophy, preached by the preachers of *Utility*—to what atrocities and absurdities might not the lustre and authority of such names give a pernicious colouring? Mr. Mill is not the only one of the new school of Utility who has misapplied the principle to the degradation of one half the human race. Another philosopher of the new school, Mr. Dumont of Geneva, another retrograde disciple of the great master of Legislation, though the collator and editor in French of Mr. Bentham's manuscripts, unites with the author of the "Article on Government" in his contemptuous exclusion of women. In the "Tactiques des Assemblées Legislatives," vol. 1. Ch. on the "*Admission of Strangers*," page 246, this lover of equal justice recommends, *with great sorrow*, the exclusion of women from even listening to legislative debates;

as is sagely done by what is called the Lower House of British Legislators—whence the extreme benignity of their laws and manners to women—lest female blandishments should distract the young orators! Such is the wisdom of Mr. Dumont on the subject of women. Does Mr. Bentham approve of such puerilities?—He laughs at them.

I therefore looked upon every day as lost till the rude gauntlet thrown down against half mankind was snatched up, and the inroad of barbarism, under the guise of philosophy, into the nineteenth century, was arrested. Weary of waiting, the protest of at least one man and one woman is here put forward against doctrines which disgrace the principle of utility: the facts are denied, and the inferences controverted, even if the facts were true. Could any thing bring the principle of utility, or the search of the greatest amount of preponderant good, into disrepute, it would be the peculiarly inconsistent conduct in its abettors, of assuming the air of dogmatizing, and expecting that opinions should be believed, without proof, without reasons, on the faith of their wisdom. Of all reasoners, he that rests on the basis of utility is the least excused in advancing new opinions, or opinions on the truth of which great interests depend, without plainly stating the grounds of his opinions. Advocates as we are of the principle of Utility as the only test of morals, conduct so disgraceful to its admirers we will not follow.

You look forward, as I do, to a state of society very different from that which now exists, in which the effort of all is to out wit, supplant, and snatch from each other; where interest is systematically opposed to duty; where the so-called system of morals is little more than a mass of hypocrisy preached by knaves, unpractised by them, to keep their slaves, male as well as female, in blind uninquiring obedience; and where the whole motley fabric is kept together by fear and blood. You look forward to a better aspect of society, where the principle of benevolence shall supersede that of fear; where restless and anxious individual competition shall give place to mutual co-operation and joint possession; where individuals in large numbers, male and female, forming voluntary associations, shall become a mutual guarantee to each other for the supply of all useful wants, and form an unsalaried and uninsolvent insurance company against all insurable casualties; where perfect freedom of opinion and perfect equality will reign amongst the co-operators; and where the children of all will be equally educated and provided for by the whole, even these children longer the slaves of individual caprice.

In truth, under the present arrangements of society, the principle of individual competition remaining, as it is, the master-key and moving principle of the whole social organization, *individual* wealth the great object sought after by all, and the quantum of happiness of each individual (other things being equal) depending on the quantum of wealth, the means of happiness, possessed by each; it seems impossible—even were all unequal legal and unequal moral restraints removed, and were no secret current of force or influence exerted to baffle new regulations of equal justice—that women should attain to equal happiness with men. Two circumstances—permanent inferiority of strength, and occasional loss of time in gestation and rearing infants—must eternally render the average exertions of women in the race of the competition for wealth less successful than those of men. The pleasant compensation that men now affect to give for these two natural sources of inferior accumulation of wealth on the part of women (aggravated a thousand degrees by their exclusions from knowledge and almost all means of useful exertions, (the very lowest only excepted), is the existing system of marriage; under which, for the mere faculty of eating, breathing and living, in whatever degree of comfort husbands may think fit, women are reduced to domestic slavery, without will of their own, or power of locomotion, otherwise than as permitted by their respective masters.

While these two natural impediments in the way of the production or accumulation of wealth, and of course of the independence and equal enjoyments of women, exist—and exist they must—it should seem that the present arrangements of society, founded on individual competition, and of course allowing of no real compensation for these impediments, are absolutely irreconcilable with the equality, in point of the command of enjoyments, of women with men. Were all partial restraints, were unequal laws and unequal morals removed, were all the means and careers of all species of knowledge and exertion equally open to both sexes; still the barriers of physical organization must, under the system of individual competition, keep depressed the average station of women beneath that of men. Though in point of knowledge, talent, and virtue, they might become their equals; in point of independence *arising from wealth* they must, under the present principle of social arrangements, remain inferior.

No doubt, so much the more dastardly appears the baseness of man, that not satisfied with these indisputable advantages of organization in the pursuit of happiness on his own theatre of free competition, he paralyses to impotence even those means which Nature has given his feebler competitor, nor ceases his oppression till he has made her his slave. The more physical advantages Nature has given man, the *less* excusable is he in superadding factitious advantages, by the abuse of strength, to those which are natural and unavoidable. Were he generous, were he just, knew he how to promote his own happiness, he would be anxious to afford *compensations* for these physical inconveniences, instead of aggravating them; that he might raise woman to a perfect equality in all things with himself, and enjoy the highest pleasures of which his nature is susceptible—those of freedom, of voluntary association amongst perfect equals. Perhaps out of the system of "Association" or "Mutual Co-operation" such happiness is not to be expected.

But I hear you indignantly reject the boon of equality with such creatures as men now are. With you I would equally elevate both sexes. Really enlightened women, disdaining equally the submissive tricks of the slave and the caprices of the despot, breathing freely only in the air of the esteem of equals, and of mutual, *unbought, uncommanded,* affection, would find it difficult to meet with associates worthy of them in men as now formed, full of ignorance and vanity, priding themselves on a *sexual* superiority, entirely independent of any merit, any superior qualities, or pretensions to them, claiming respect from the strength of their arm and the lordly faculty of producing beards attached by nature to their chins! No: unworthy of, as incapable of appreciating, the delight of the society of such women, are the great majority of the existing race of men. The pleasures of mere animal appetite, the pleasures of commanding (the prettier and more helpless the slave, the greater these pleasures of the brute), are the only pleasures which the majority of men seek for from women, are the only pleasures which their education and the hypocritical system of morals with which they have been necessarily imbued, permit them to expect. To wish for the fragrance of the rose, we must have an organization capable of receiving pleasure from it, and must be persuaded that such lovely flowers as roses exist. To wish for the enjoyment of the higher pleasures of sympathy and communication of knowledge between the sexes, heightened by that mutual grace and glow, that decorum and mutual respect, to which the feeling of perfect, unrestrained equality in the intercourse gives birth, a man must have heard of such pleasures, must be able to conceive them, and must have an organization from nature or education, or both, capable of receiving delight from them when presented to him. To enjoy these pleasures, to which their other pleasures, a few excepted, are but the play of children or brutes, the bulk of men want a sixth sense; they want the capacity of feeling them, and of believing that such things are in nature to be found. A mole cannot enjoy the " beauties and glories" (as a Professor terms them) of the visible world ; nor can brute men enjoy the intellectual and sympathetic pleasures of equal intercourse with women, such as some are, such as all might be. Real and comprehensive knowledge, physical and moral, equally and impartially given by education and by all other means to both sexes, is the key to such higher enjoyments.

Even under the present arrangements of society, founded as they all are on the basis of individual competition, nothing could be more easy than to put the *rights* of women, political and civil, on a perfect equality with those of men. It is only to abolish all prohibitory and exclusive laws, —statute or what are called " common,"—the remnants of the barbarous customs of our ignorant ancestors; particularly the horrible and odious inequality and indissolubility of that disgrace of civilization, the present marriage code. Women then might exert in a free career with men their faculties of mind and body, to whatever degree developed, in pursuit of happiness by means of exertion, as men do. But this would not raise women to an equality of happiness with men : their rights might be equal, but not their happiness, because unequal powers under free competition must produce unequal effects.

In truth, the system of the most enlightened of the school of those reformers called political economists, is still founded on exclusions. Its basis is too narrow for human happiness. A more comprehensive system, founded on equal benevolence, on the true developement of the principle of Utility, is wanting. Let the *competitive* political economists be satisfied with the praise of causing the removal of some of the rubbish of ignorant restrictions, under the name of laws, impeding the developement of human exertion in the production of wealth. To build up a new fabric of social happiness, comprehending equally the interests of all existing human beings, has never been contemplated by them, and is altogether beyond the scope of their little theories ; aiming at the utmost at increasing the number of what they style the happy middling orders, but leaving the great bulk of human beings to eternal ignorance and toil, requited by the mere means of prolonging from day to day an unhealthy and precarious existence. To a new science, the *social science,* or the science of promoting human happiness, that of political economy, or the mere science of producing wealth by individual competition, must give way.

As one of the preliminary measures to this great end, let us proceed to lay to rest the presumptuous anathema of the "Article on Government" against half the human race.

CONTENTS.

Introductory Letter to Mrs. Wheeler . . . . *page* v

PART I.
Examination of the general argument of the "Article on Government" for political rights 1

PART II.
Application of this argument to the case of women . . . 21

QUESTION 1. Does an identity or an involving of interest, in point of fact and of necessity, exist between women and men? 25
    Case of women without husbands or fathers . . . 27
    —— of adult daughters 34
    —— of wives 54

QUESTION 2. If this involving of the interests of women in those of men do exist, is it a sufficient reason, or any reason at all, that either of the parties, men or women, with interests so identified, should therefore be deprived of civil or political rights? 114
    Reasons in favor of the exclusive exercise of political rights by women 127
    Reasons in favor of the exclusive exercise of political rights by men 128

QUESTION 3. Is there in the nature of things any security for equality of enjoyments, proportioned to exertion and capabilities, but by means of equal civil rights? or any security for equal civil but by means of equal political rights? . . . 152

Equal *civil* and *criminal* laws are requisite to secure to women equal chances of enjoyment with men 155
Equal *political* laws are requisite to secure to women equal civil and criminal laws, and through them equal enjoyments, with men 166
Concluding Address to Women 187
Index 213

APPEAL,

&c.

PART I.

EXAMINATION OF THE *GENERAL* ARGUMENT OF THE "ARTICLE ON GOVERNMENT," FOR POLITICAL RIGHTS.

TOPICS OF PART I.

1. The general argument of the "Article" for Human Rights, is founded on the universal love of power of all human beings over all their fellow-creatures, for selfish purposes. This is stated to be the grand governing law of human nature. 2

2. But, if in the disposition of one half the human race, men, an exception from this grand governing law exist towards the other half, women, what becomes of the law itself and the arguments founded on it? 8

3. Still more if the alleged law is relinquished, as by the "Article" it is, as to the disposition of men towards *three fourths* of the race, children as well as women, the law itself and the argument founded on it, must fall. 10

4. This alleged primary law of human nature, is, however, but a secondary law, operating under peculiar and ill-arranged circumstances only. 12

5. The primary law of human nature operating equally under all circumstances, is simply the desire of happiness, or love of pleasure, and aversion to pain. 13

6. The affecting to include and merge the interests of three fourths of the human race in that of the one fourth, arises altogether from want of sympathy towards the excluded three fourths. . 14

7. Claims of women to political rights—along with those of children—are contemptuously dismissed by the "Article," in six lines! 16

8. Reasons for exclusion of children from political rights, are different from, and altogether inapplicable to, those regarding women. 18

9. Mode of conducting the argument of the 2nd Part; in opposition to the pretended identification or involving of the interests of women in those of men. 19

PART I.

EXAMINATION OF THE *GENERAL* ARGUMENT OF THE "ARTICLE ON GOVERNMENT," FOR POLITICAL RIGHTS.

AT the head of moral, including political, philosophy, in Britain, stands Mr. Bentham. His celebrated works, "*Traités de Legislation,*" "*Theorie des Peines et des Recompenses,*" "*Tactiques des Assemblées Legislatives,*" "*Preuves Judiciaires,*" edited in French by Mr. Dumont of Geneva; with the "Introduction to Morals and Legislation," "Essay on Usury," on "Government," on "Prison, Discipline," and various other important Works published by himself in English, have procured for him this high pre-eminence. Amongst the most eminent of his disciples and admirers, is Mr. Mill, the author of the *History of British India*. Mr. Mill, one of the most successful advocates of the doctrine of *Utility,* as the test of Morals, as established by Mr. Bentham, has written several excellent articles on this basis, in the *Supplement to the Encyclopedia Britannica.* Many of these have been reprinted, in a separate form, for circulation, but not for sale. Amongst these articles, the most important, perhaps, is that on " Government."

As far as the simplest political rights of *man* are concerned, Mr. Mill is entitled to the thanks of all men, for the plain and unanswerable statements and reasonings in this "Article," by which he has shown what those rights ought to be, in order to promote the greatest possible quantity of happiness to all men. But, is it not strange that a philosopher, a lover of wisdom, avowedly founding his arguments on Utility,—that is to say, on the tendency of actions or institutions to promote the greatest possible quantity of human happiness,—should deliberately, in the very threshold of his argument, put aside *one half* the human race, of all ages and all characters and conditions, as unentitled to consideration; to any further consideration at least than such as may arise from the coincidence of their welfare with that of the more fortunate half which he takes under his philosophic protection. The half of the human race, whose happiness Mr. Mill takes under his protection, is that half—is it necessary to say?—to which he has the good fortune to belong.

Were Mr. Mill's system of philosophy founded on the assumption that *man* was naturally and necessarily a beneficent being, always inclined to promote the happiness of those within his power, and necessarily acquainted with the means to promote this end in a degree superior to that possessed by those over whom his power extended; however fond and puerile we might conceive the assumption, the *inference*, that power over others might be safely placed in his hands, would be at least fairly drawn from the premises.

But, strange to say, the assumption, on which the whole fabric of Mr. Mill's philosophy rests, is directly opposed to any such notion of natural beneficence and unerring judgment on the part of men. Mr. Mill's philosophical basis of reasoning is, that *all* men are necessarily inclined to use for their own exclusive advantage whatever power they can acquire over the actions of their fellow-men, and that the more knowledge they happen to possess,

founded on universal *Love of Power for selfish Purposes.* 5

with the more skill will they use this power to promote such exclusive interest, at the expense of those over whom their power extends.

In proof of this position, read the following passages in the *Supplement to the Encycl. Brit.*

Page 494. " That one human being will desire to render " the person and property of another subservient to his " pleasures, notwithstanding the pain or loss of pleasure " which it may occasion to that other individual, is the " foundation of Government. The desire of the object " implies the desire of the power necessary to accomplish " the object. The desire, therefore, of that power which is " necessary to render the persons and properties of human " beings subservient to our pleasures, is a grand governing " law of human nature."

Page 494. " The demand therefore of power over the " acts of other men" (human beings) " is really boundless. " It is boundless in two ways ; boundless in the number " of persons to whom we would extend it, and boundless " in its degree over the actions of each."

Page 495. " We have thus arrived at several con- " clusions of the highest possible importance. We have " seen that the very principle of human nature upon which " the necessity of Government is founded, the propensity " of one man to possess himself of the objects of desire at " the cost of another, leads on by infallible sequence, where " power over a community is attained and nothing checks, " not only to that degree of plunder which leaves the mem- " bers (excepting always the recipients and instruments of " the plunder) the bare means of subsistence, but to that " degree of cruelty which is necessary to keep in existence " the most intense terror."

Page 496. "It is proved therefore by the closest deduc-
"tion from the acknowledged laws of human nature, and
"by direct and decisive experiments, that the ruling one
"or the ruling few, would, if checks did not operate in the
"way of prevention, reduce the great mass of the people
"subject to their power, at least to the condition of
"negroes in the West Indies."

It is true that towards the end of the "Article," an admission is made, which would go far to invalidate the general principle. It is this: page 505, *Suppl.* "It will be said
"that a conclusion ought not to be drawn from the un-
"thinking conduct of the great majority of an aristocratical
"body against the capability of such a body for acting
"wisely" (in a way to promote the universal interest?) "in
"the management of public affairs; because the body will
"always contain a certain proportion of wise men, and the
"rest will be governed by them. Nothing but this can be
"said with pertinency. And, under certain modifications,
"this may be said with truth. The *wise* and *good* in any
"class of men, do, to all general purposes, govern the rest."

In this passage it is evident that too much is admitted. The wise, doubtless, the knowing ones, in all classes of men, do govern the rest, because they more effectually promote the apparent interests of the whole body. If by the *good* be meant those who prefer the universal interest to that of themselves or of the body to which they belong, universal experience coincides with all the previous positions of the "Article" in disproving the assertion. The word *good*—if it were designed to mean any more than those who are kindly disposed in their private concerns—(and even, with such meaning, it would be inaccurate) seems to have crept inadvertently into this passage.

founded on universal *Love of Power for selfish Purposes.* 7

On the whole, then, it is clear that the basis of the reasoning of the "Article" is the position that, *the demand of power of all human beings over their fellow-creatures, where not restrained by checks, is boundless, as well in the number of persons over whom it would extend, as in its degree over the actions of each*; *and would reduce each and all, if unrestrained, at least to the condition of negroes in the West Indies.* Such is stated to be the *grand governing law of human nature.*

Still, however, in the face of this grand governing law of human nature, this male philosopher maintains, that, with respect to *one half* the human race, women, this universal disposition of man to use power for his own exclusive benefit ceases, and his knowledge with respect to them, invariably shows him that their happiness coincides with his, and is included in it! This exception of one half from the influence of the general rule of the disposition to misuse power, is certainly a pretty large exception, requiring all the boldness of an English philosopher. In any other hands, so large an exception would go far to destroy the rule. An exception of one half! add one to one half, one out of a hundred millions of human beings, and the rule will be at the other-side, on the side of the beneficent exertion of power; and what would then become of the basis of the argument for human rights as founded on the inclination to use power for the exclusive benefit of the possessor? The rule would become the exception; beneficence would become the adjunct of power; and the argument for restraints on the use of power, or against the intrusting of power to one individual over the actions of his fellows, must be abandoned.

And who knows after all that can be said, on which

side the majority of human beings lies? on the side of the misuse, or of the beneficent use of power? on the side of that half of the human family who have the honor to reckon the vote of the philosopher in their favor, or on the side of the other half whose interests he surrenders to the power and humanity of himself and his associates? It is certainly *as* possible that the neglected half may form the majority of adult rational beings, as that the favored half may be the majority. To this state of uncertainty must such an exception reduce this argument in favor of human rights and human happiness! To an equal chance of truth or falsehood, to a matter of eternal doubt and disputation, its *probative force* always the smallest possible, depending on the balance of a die! If absolute enumeration of the two halves of human kind, should hereafter show the excluded half to be the majority, Mr. Mill's basis of just government would be overturned; and in the mean time, it would rest on no firmer foundation than that of possibility, of a mere equality of chances.

Having laid down such a basis for political rights, as the necessary tendency to the use of power for the exclusive benefit of its possessors, in favor of all *men* whose happiness may be affected by such power; in what way does the "Article" seek to evade the equal claims of the other half of the human race, women, to similar protection against the abuses of the same power? We may conceive three modes by which it may be sought to evade the application of the general principle of security to women. It may be boldly said, that they are incapable of becoming rational and susceptible of happiness like men. Secondly, it may be said, that whether capable or not, men being equally numerous, are the stronger half of the species, and should therefore render women, like any other objects of desire, tributary to their enjoyment. Or, thirdly, by a more refined sophistry, it may be allowed, that though women are capable of rationality and enjoyment equally with men, though their happiness should be kept in view as a primary object as much as that of men, the other half of the race; yet is all restraint on the power of men quite superfluous as to them, inasmuch as, *in their case,* men are not influenced by the general tendency of their unenlightened natures to misuse power, but necessarily include the happiness of women in all speculations and regulations as to their own happiness.

Let us see which of these three evasions of his own principle, his grand, governing, primary, law of human nature, Mr. Mill has adopted.

The Article on Government asserts, page 500, *Suppl. to Enc. Brit.* "One thing is pretty clear, that all those indivi-
" duals whose interests are indisputably included in those of
" other individuals, may be struck off" (from political rights)
"without inconvenience. In this light may be viewed all
" children up to a certain age, whose interests are in-
"volved in those of their parents. In this light, also, women
" may be regarded, the interest of almost all of whom is
" involved either in that of their fathers or in that of their
" husbands."

Thus cavalierly are dealt with by this philosopher of humanity, the interests of one half the human species! Not so Mr. Bentham, whose disciple he is: the philosophy of that enlightened and benevolent man, embraces in its grasp every sentient human being, and acknowledges the claim of every rational adult, without distinction of sex or colour, to equal political rights. Is the authority of the disciple above that of the master? We shall discard both: and on the great principle of *Utility* admitted by both, by both appealed to as the test of political as well as private morals, proceed to investigate the propositions before us.

One half of the human race in almost all countries, (in countries very rapidly increasing in population, or where from wretchedness the mean duration of life is very low, much more than one half) are under twenty or twenty-one years of age, their faculties not fully developed, not capable of performing all the duties, or exercising all the rights, of the fully-formed portion of the population. Of the adult half of the human race, one half again consists of men, the other of women. In some countries, as well as in particular districts, it appears that the proportion of the sexes varies; but in general, equality is pretty nearly preserved in the relative numbers. According to Mr. Mill's most enlarged view therefore, one fourth of the human race, or of any portion thereof, is the greatest number whose interests ought to be directly consulted in the making of laws, the interests of the other three fourths being, somehow or other, benevolently included in those of the stronger ruling quarter; though this same quarter, in the exercise of its powers towards its own members, would, if uncontrolled by restraint, infallibly misuse these powers to the exclusive advantage of whatever number less than the whole might become possessed of them. The ruling quarter is necessarily benevolent towards the three fourths, but as necessarily malevolent towards all the members of the fourth to which it belongs! Or, if benevolence towards the three fourths be discarded, another supposition as strange must be made, to wit, that nature has, to save man the trouble of thought or the need of sympathy towards three fourths of his race, so mysteriously and indissolubly amalgamated their pleasures, pains, and wishes, with his, that it is impossible for him to promote the happiness of the one without at the same time promoting that of the others! The grandest moral discovery this that ever has been made! a discovery superseding with respect to the interests of three fourths of the human race, the necessity of study or of the acquisition of habits of sympathy. The discovery of earlier times—for so many dreary centuries reverenced—was, that the possession of power by one or by a few, tens, or hundreds, or thousands, necessarily amalgamated their interest with that of all under the influence of their power; caused the one to be *included* in the other, and necessarily inspired such knowledge and benevolence into the possessors of power as rendered them the fittest instruments for promoting the happiness of all. Mr. Mill has discovered all this to be false philosophy, belied by every page of history, by the occurrences of every day. But, increase the number of the governing party to one fourth or nearly one fourth, and let that one fourth be the division to which the philosopher himself happens to belong, and he finds the philosophy admirable. The ignorance of men possessing power, is changed into knowledge; their love of exclusive interest, into benevolence. The power that is necessarily mischievous as applied to any of the members of the favored fourth, becomes as necessarily good when applied to the excluded three fourths. Wonderful alchemy of modern philosophy in the hand of such a magician! If he could but as easily change the dispositions of the possessors of power towards the one fourth, as he takes credit for having done towards the hapless three fourths, who so worthy as he of apotheosis!

But the truth is, that all such quibbling and vain distinctions are unworthy the name of philosophy. Men without knowledge or benevolence, or placed in such circumstances as are ordinarily incompatible with the exercise of such qualities, will necessarily use power for their own apparent exclusive benefit, at the expense of all other sentient beings, children, women, or other men, whose interests may *appear* to them incompatible with their own. Nor is there any mysterious identification or inclusion of the interests of the weak and ignorant with those of the strong and knowing. On the contrary, the more ignorant and the more weak—whether from nature in the case of children, or from nature as to weakness, and from privation of education and stultifying institutions as to knowledge, in the case of women—the less will there be, or appear to be, of identification or inclusion of interests; because the less of resemblance, of equality, the less there will be of sympathy; the less power to resist and the less of controul, the greater will be the temptation to, the more infallible will be the certainty of, abuse of power.

But it does not appear that Mr. Mill has laid a sufficiently broad basis for the great argument on which the institution of government ought to depend, in order to promote the greatest possible quantity of happiness to those influenced by it. It would appear that Mr. Mill's alleged primary principle of human nature, is but a *secondary* principle, and dependant on particular conditions. It is not true that all men are inclined to use power for their own exclusive benefit. It is not true that all men are in-

Love of Pleasure and Aversion to Pain. 13

clined to use power beneficently, so as to calculate the effect of its exercise on the happiness of all to be affected by it. The original principle of human nature is neither the one nor the other of these two: it is simply the desire of happiness and aversion to misery, without any wish, kindly or malignant, to others. As men acquire knowledge, and become surrounded, in the course of barbarism or civilization, by circumstances conciliating their happiness with, or putting it in opposition to, that of their fellow-creatures, they pursue to a greater or less extent their own individual happiness in connexion with, or to the exclusion of, that of others. It is neither an original, nor an universal, principle of human beings, to trample on, any more than it is to promote, the happiness of others. It is never trampled on but when rightly, or erroneously judged to be incompatible with the happiness of the agent. The two conditions requisite to the truth of Mr. Mill's proposition, as to the tendency to the abuse or misuse of power, are, that the persons possessing power shall, from the operation of circumstances, be shut out from the moral knowledge requisite to show them the identity of their real comprehensive interest with that of their fellow-creatures, and shall also be divested of those dispositions or habits of sympathy necessary to enable them to act according to their knowledge. With such knowledge and dispositions, no restraints on power would be wanting: and such knowledge and dispositions are certainly *possible*. It is as certainly true that the very possession of power without restraint, is in almost every instance sufficient to confound knowledge and eradicate sympathy where they previously existed, or to prevent their formation. These modifications seem to be requisite to render universal

Mr. Mill's secondary principle of human action. Were knowledge and benevolence so increased and improved by education or otherwise—and there is no physical or moral impossibility of their being so increased and improved—that all men saw their interest in tracing the consequences of their actions on the happiness of others as well as on their own, and that they were disposed to regulate their actions by this knowledge, there would be no need of restraints, because men would not wish for power over each other: the means of influencing rational beings by the exhibition of reason, is all that would be exercised or wished for. *Under the existing and all past circumstances of society,* Mr. Mill's proposition is doubtless correct as applied to the immense majority of men: while these or similar circumstances operate upon them, men will, almost universally, use power for their own exclusive, obvious and immediate, benefit.

If it be said that the terms "grand, governing," law do not imply either primary, or universal, the meaning will be reduced to what is above explained, a mode of action occurring under given circumstances.

"Women and children!" how contemptuous the classification! weakness and ignorance the common qualities! what volumes it speaks as to the sympathy and respect of the writer for the equal capacity of enjoying, and therefore the equal right to enjoyment, of women and men! If this writer *possess* women and children, it would be curious to observe how his principles modify his conduct, whether their happiness is in his mind so identified and included in his as to be taken for the same; and whether, if so, if he use so meekly over these his dependants that almost despotic power which laws give him, such forbearance does not arise from that superior knowledge and benevolence which would lead him to exercise aright similar power, though equally unrestrained, over his fellow-men. Some examples there are, of kindness in domestic life, and brutality in the use of political power on the part of the same individual: but these are rare; and when they happen, the domestic kindness will almost always be found to be resolvable into selfishness one little step enlarged, separating not only itself but every thing honored by connexion with it, women, children, horses, and furniture, from the rest of the world out of the magic circle. Vain basis for equal enjoyments, and, as necessary to these, for civil and political rights, is the occasional and limited expansion of so sickly a plant as selfishness!

" Women, and the mob! the canaille, the profane vulgar, the swinish multitude!" Such are the associations, the terms of degradation and insult, which have passed as justificatory reasons by the possessors of power for trampling on the happiness of all the helpless of the human race, helpless whether from want of knowledge or of efficient strength. Despotism has of late smarted in Europe, for its contemptuous upbraidings of its own handy-work, the ignorance, the wretchedness, and the impotence, of the great bulk of *men*. Its tone is now changed: it insults no more: it seeks to conciliate: it allows, in words, the claim of all men to happiness, and professes an anxiety to promote that happiness. Wherefore? This impotence, of the bulk of *men*, has shown the tremendous energy of its strength; and even despotism *dares* insult no longer. The tauntings with which even despotism has ceased to revile its victims, because it begins to fear their strength guided by their knowledge, it was reserved for philosophy, the philosophy of an Englishman, to prolong towards *its* helpless victims, women, because their strength could not be feared, and from knowledge they are effectually debarred. In this at least faithful to his own philosophy—" wherever man has the power, and can exercise it with impunity, there will he not only oppress, but upbraid"—he aptly and persuasively illustrates it. *Six lines*, out of 32 pages on the principles of government, are devoted to the pretensions of women and children, or rather of children and women—for children take the precedence in this new and enlightened nomenclature—of which, two lines include the pretended principle of exclusion; two the application to children; and two more, last of all, the application to the hopelessly weak and helpless appendage to the race of man, women.

And yet, such are to be the judges in the last resort of the political rights of women; *men!* inclined by their very nature, as the "Article" maintains, to the boundless misuse of uncontrolled power till its victims are reduced at least to the condition of negroes in the West Indies. Nature has given these judges *power:* secure in the eternal possession of this power, they deem even discussion to be thrown away on those who have none to help them; and two lines written by the philosopher, of the new and most improved edition of modern moral philosophy, consigns one half the human race, one half of the adult portion of the race, to irremediable dependance on the other! the weak to dependance on the strong, on the strong without any control, on the strong who, glorying in their strength, disdain to reason with, to give any explanations for the soothing of the weak!

Had nothing been said, in this celebrated "Article" on

Government, about women, it might have been supposed that in advocating the primary political rights of man, those of women were meant to be included as forming part of the race. Room would have been left for doubt as to the object, in this respect, of this audacious and selfish abuse of the new philosophy. On so presumptuous a hope, the *veto* is placed. 'Tis not enough to neglect women in the distribution of rights; they must be put forward, and by name excluded; excluded in a sentence; excluded in the true Eastern style, without condescending to listen to their humble plea for admission, as though all consideration on the subject were superfluous; as though the writer were conscious that those only who have not strength condescend to reason!

Strength let him, and those who love to tyrannize with him, retain: but the voice of reason they must hear—they who have, in their own case, set the example of so freely using it. There are, even amongst men, those who spurn the selfishness of such exclusive doctrines; who have never felt pleasure in making the will of others bend slavishly, without persuasion, to theirs; who have never felt delight in society, except in that of unconstrained equals. It is for them to protest and clear themselves from liability to the disgraceful imputation of seeking to build their rights and happiness on the prostration of the rights and happiness of one half of their fellow-creatures.

The claim of children to protection from the laws against those in whose power they are placed, we are not here called upon to discuss. Enough to observe that, the supposition of an identity of interest (in the common acceptation of the term, interest) between them and men, is a mere fiction, or in other words a falsehood—or why the necessity of regulations, as society advances in improvement, to protect children from the abuse of power on the part of their parents?—therefore this, like all other legal or philosophical fictions, cannot be a just reason for excluding children from political rights. There are reasons, nevertheless, and good ones, for this exclusion; but such as would not apply to the adult portion of the race, to women; and therefore not such as would suit the purpose of the philosopher of the *human race* in his laudable desire of building his system of liberty on the political, civil, and therefore the social and domestic, slavery of one half of his kind. In order to include women in the proscription of children, a fiction must be manufactured— as none of the good reasons applicable to children would be found to apply to women; and this romance of an *identity of interest* is the ingenious, say rather the vulgar, the audacious, fiction devised. From want of developement of their powers, from an *inevitable* defect of knowledge, from an incapability of equal co-operation to the common happiness or of equal enjoyment, from the impotence of even providing for their own wants, and consequently from the impossibility of their using political power for their own benefit or that of others, are children, as a matter of regret and of necessity, to be excluded from political, and many civil, rights, until, and only until, their corporeal and mental faculties can by use and education be so fully developed as to enable them to act and think, to co-operate and enjoy, like the fully developed portion of their race. None of these or any such useful considerations would serve the purpose of radical, any more than of single or many-handed, despotism: they are therefore passed by; and a fiction is called in to support exclusion; falsehood, on which injustice may repose! Oh! admirable foundation! worthy of such a superstructure!

From this examination it results, that the pretext set up to exclude women from political rights, namely, the inclination of men to use power over them beneficently, would, if admitted, sweep away the grand argument itself for the political rights of men; inasmuch as it would prove men to be inclined to use power, though without limits or checks, *beneficently*, over at least half their race. Whence the argument founded on the contrary supposition, that of the universal love of power for *selfish* purposes, must fall. The penalty of injustice to women is, therefore, the justification, by the most simple and unanswerable reasoning, of similar injustice from men to men.

Let the "Article" allow, then, the claims of women, or, in fair reasoning, relinquish those of men, to protection from the misuse of political, and thence of all other, power.

Dismissing then the case of children, which would form a separate discussion, we shall investigate the philosophical pretext of the "Article" for the degradation of one half of the adult portion of the human race, in the following order.

1. Does this identity of interest between men and women, in point of fact, and of necessity, exist?
2. If it do exist, is it a sufficient cause, or any reason at all, why either of the parties, with interests thus identified, should therefore be deprived of political rights?
3. Is there in the nature of things any security for equality of enjoyments proportioned to exertion and capabilities, but by means of equal civil

rights? or any security for equal civil, but by means of equal political, rights?

In the course of this discussion, the numerous false statements and errors of reasoning, as they appear to us, involved in the two-line proscription, by the "Article," of one half the human race, will fall under review. We could have pardoned the advocate of despotism, who trampled on the rights of all, for involving women in the proscription: but we must be excused for protesting against so gross a misapplication of the principle of Utility as that before us, which, under the garb of reason, turns recreant to its own principles, and capriciously divides the human race into two moral masses, the one of which is to be saturated with liberty and enjoyment, the other with slavery, privation, and insult.

PART II.

APPLICATION OF THIS ARGUMENT TO THE CASE OF WOMEN.

QUESTION I.—*Does an identity, or an involving, of interest, in point of fact and of necessity, exist between women and men?*

TOPICS OF QUESTION I.

Hitherto, other grounds than those of the "Article on Government" have been put forward to justify the withholding of political rights from women. The "Article" limits them to *one*; namely, "a supposed identity, or involving, of interest between certain classes of women and certain classes of men." . . . . *page* 25

There are three great classes, or divisions, of women, whose interests or happiness are to be considered. 27

    First, All women without husbands or fathers.
    Second, Adult daughters within their fathers' establishments.
    Third, Wives.

    I. The first, the unconnected, insultingly called the unprotected, class of women, those without husbands or fathers, consist of, 1, all such adult young women previous to marriage; 2, all women who never marry; and 3, widows.

    —Are *their* interests involved in the interests of any men whatever? 27

Meaning of the mysterious terms, "involving of interest," made use of as the basis of exclusion: it can only refer to immediate everyday interests: resumed page 45, where treating of adult daughters. 28

The first and obvious error of the reasoning of the "Article" against women, is, that "although it affirms that only a *part* of women find their interest involved in those of men, it yet excludes *all* women from political rights, as well those whose interests are involved as those whose interests it admits not to be involved." 28

The "Article" does not pretend that they are involved; and therefore gives no reason for excluding any of these, of the first division, from political rights: they are on the contrary much more in need of the protection of political rights and of equal laws than a class of men. 32

II. The second class or division are, adult daughters within their fathers' establishments.—Are *their* interests involved in those of their fathers? 34

An exception which the "Article" will admit, is the case of *illegitimate* daughters, whose interests are clearly not involved in those of their fathers. 35

Similarity of organization and enjoyments leads to greater sympathy, thence to more involving of interests between adult sons than between adult daughters, and their fathers: yet sons are not on that account deprived of political rights. 38

Similarity of active pursuits, of arts and sciences, between sons and fathers, leads to the same results. 39

Circumstances render it the interest, and therefore the wish, of daughters, as soon as adult, to leave their fathers' home, and name, and seek new connexions: so completely *unidentified*, in the present state of social arrangements, are their interests with those of their fathers. 40

The interests of adult daughters are much more involved in those of their mothers than their fathers, from similarity of leading circumstances in the condition of both. 42

Even the laws, in these, as in most civilized, countries, recognize an *opposition* of interests between adult daughters, as well as between adult sons, and their fathers, by taking away from the parent all direct control over the actions of children of age, equally, whether sons or daughters. 45

Great confusion of ideas as to the meaning of the terms, "identity or involving of interests." 46

'Tis only in a few points of grosser interest that the individuals of every family, sons as well as daughters, are identified as against all other families and individuals. 48

The isolated, antisocial, *family interest*, must be distinguished from the *individual interest* of the members of the family, particularly of the adult daughters. 48

The only sense in which the terms, identity or involving of interests, can be with any propriety used, is to denote the probability of better treatment—shared in with all the members of a family, servants, and animals—to be expected from prosperity of masters. In this sense only, though their relative situation were as abject as that of cats, may the interests of adult daughters be said to be involved in that of the masters, their fathers. 49

Summary respecting state of adult daughters. 52

Qu. 1.]   Topics of Question the First.   23

III. The third class or division of women, are, wives.—Are *their* interests involved in those of their husbands? . . 54

The ex-parte marriage code, absurdly called the marriage contract, partakes no more of the nature of contracts than slave-codes, or any other codes of law made without the consent of those whose happiness they affect 55

The great mass of women, under actual circumstances, must submit to them or starve. 57

Although women, like men, as soon as adult, are in most civilized countries protected in civil and personal rights, against their fathers as against other individuals; yet, no sooner are they married, than by the marriage code, notwithstanding their experience, they are again deprived of all these inefficient rights, and thrown back into the class of children or idiots. 58

Disgusting falsehood of the pretext, that the legal despotism of man in marriage, is neutralized by his dependence on his wife for sexual pleasures. 60

Neither by law, nor opinion, nor practice, is the husband dependent on the wife for such pleasures. 62

But, by law, by opinion, and in practice, the wife is entirely dependent on the husband for them. 64

The marriage codes of all nations, even the most civilized, render women in effect the slaves of men.—Definition of a slave. . . 66

Men under similar circumstances would esteem themselves slaves. 67

Real evils of slavery the same, whether endured or inflicted by women or men. 68

Domestic despotism corrupts man's moral frame. 70

Marriage vow of slavery is an insult, as needless as cruel. . . 71

Slavery of the wife would not be justified even if it promoted the happiness of the husband. 73

Involving of interests must mean that the one enjoys as much as the other. Is this true as between husbands and wives? . . 75

First, as to the pleasures of the senses. So notoriously are wives and all women restrained, that equal enjoyment of these pleasures with men, particularly eating and drinking, is esteemed *immoral* in them, while to men it is freely permitted. Sexual pleasures, in husbands, no punishment at all; in wives, punishment, legal and moral, only short of death. 77

Other pleasures of the senses of the wife, as of the eye, the ear, mostly enjoyed in association with other pleasures intellectual or sympathetic, are entirely under the control of the husband: the rule is privation: the exception is, occasional permission, as to children, to enjoy. 79

From intellectual pleasures even with their husbands and families wives are excluded by defect of education and contempt of the stronger and more improved sex. From social pleasures, those of sympathy and free intercourse, like men, with their fellow-creatures, male and female, at home and abroad, the marriage-code right of imprisonment in the hands of the husband, effectually cuts them off. 80

In social and intellectual, as in all sensual pleasures, the husband is entirely unrestrained by the wife. Even her remonstrance is presumption: she has been compelled to vow to *obey*. 82

Permitted pleasures, though equal, would not give wives equal happiness with husbands. The want of voluntariness, or self-command, would still keep them at an immeasurable distance, in point of enjoyment, from their husbands. 89

The uncertainty also of the continuance of the enjoyments of the wife, though equal while they lasted, to those of the husband, the vicissitudes to which all wives are exposed, and from which husbands are exempted, still further sink the lot of wives in the scale of happiness. 92

That dissimilarity of organization which is not connected with sexual enjoyment, not only indisposes men to promote the happiness of their wives equally with their own, were they ever so well inclined; but renders it more difficult for them to do so. . . . 93

The very assumption of despotic power by husbands over wives, is itself a demonstration that in the opinion of husbands, a contrariety, and not an involving, of interests, exists between them and their wives. 98

Were such the order of nature, that in the human race, as in the eagle tribe and amongst some other animals, the female had been formed the stronger animal; what would man have thought of woman's justice, had she deprived him of political rights? . . . 99

These general facts are not weakened by the occasional permitted contentment, or even equal enjoyments, with their husbands, under peculiar circumstances, of some married women. 101

Summary of the argument of this first question as to the involving of interests. 107

PART II.

APPLICATION OF THIS ARGUMENT TO THE CASE OF WOMEN.

QUESTION I.—*Does an identity, or an involving, of interest, in point of fact and of necessity, exist between women and men?*

THE first point to be settled with the "Article" is the matter of fact which it assumes as the basis of the argument; " Does this identity of interest between men and women, in point of fact, and of necessity, exist?" If not, women ought, according to Mr. Mill's philosophy, to be admitted to an equality of political, as well as of civil and social, rights and enjoyments with men.

Other grounds for the exclusion of women from political rights have been taken by other men, enjoying the names of moralists, philosophers, statesmen. Of these Mr. Mill has not availed himself: he has passed them by, doubtless because he thought them futile and untenable. Where men have condescended to give any reasons for the exclusion of half their race from civil or political rights, those reasons have been such as the following;—general inferiority of muscular powers (strength) and stature on the part of women, general inferiority of the higher intellectual powers, judgement and reasoning, frequent incapacity of exercising even these limited powers from child-bearing and its consequences, consequent inaptitude of women to the performance of many important offices, the supposed necessity of cultivating to the utmost, for mutual happiness, a diversity of character in the two sexes. These, and such reasons, sometimes, and but of late years—since it has become necessary to give or to invent any reasons at all for oppression—have been given: for, until lately, antipathy and ignorance have been in the habit of alleging their feelings, precedent, nature, and such like terms, to justify whatever exclusions or regulations they thought proper to adopt. Some no doubt, anxious to establish political rights for the male part, or even a considerable portion of the male part, of the species, have, merely through prudence, kept back the consideration of the political rights of women, lest so large a demand on political power should lead it to throw discord between the claimants of the political rights of *men*. This motive, it may be observed, though good as to political rights, could have no place as to civil, from which the great majority of women are as much degraded, and rendered wretched, by exclusion, as from political rights; man seeming every where to solace himself for his loss of political rights by usurping from women even their civil rights, and thus turning his companion into his slave.

However this may be, we are not here called upon to examine these or any other reasons against the utility of the equal rights of women, *that* reason, only excepted, which Mr. Mill has brought forward, and on which he exclusively relies. Such an examination would lead us into an immense general question not now before us. On such an examination our present opponent would probably adopt the same side of the argument with us, as his rule of exclusion depends on the simple fact of identity of interest between men and women, or rather on the inclusion of the happiness of women in that of men. If it should turn out that the interests, or happiness, of women, are no more included in those of men than the happiness of some men, under peculiar circumstances and with favorable dispositions, is identified with that of some others, Mr. Mill will admit that no ground is left for the exclusion of women from political or civil rights; and also most probably, that all the reasons set up to exclude them will be found to be reasons the most unanswerable for shielding them with every civil and political protection of the law, at least equal to those who have the physical power of oppressing them.

" Is then," to use Mr. Mill's words, " the interest of al-"most all women involved either in that of their fathers " or in that of their husbands ?"

There are three great classes or divisions of women, whose situation requires to be separately considered.

All women without husbands or fathers.
Adult daughters in their fathers' establishments.
Wives.

I. With the case of those women who have neither husbands nor fathers, we begin.

It would be difficult perhaps to propose a phrase better calculated for the purposes of sophistry than this of " the involving of interests." It may be fairly put abreast with the exploded sophistry of " virtual representation." Comprehensively considered, and supposing every individual possessed of perfect wisdom and benevolence, the interests of all individuals, male and female, are involved in or identified with those of others, or of each other. Or, in other words, more happiness would be produced to all, if every one endeavored in all his actions to produce the greatest result of happiness, whether to himself or to others. But, in the actual state of things, individuals are not perfectly wise or benevolent: in the actual state of things, *circumstances* conceal from individuals their real comprehensive interest, and render it indispensable for every one to pursue his own exclusive good, though at the expense of the greater good of others. The interests here in question, are not those of the comprehensive moral, or philosophical, class, but those of every-day life and of vulgar pursuit. These immediate, apparent, interests, the "Article" maintains, must, from the primary law of their nature, be exclusively pursued by all men having power, over their fellow-creatures, and at their expense. The question is, is there under the actual circumstances of social arrangements, an exception to this grand governing law of human nature in the dispositions and conduct of fathers and husbands to their adult daughters and wives respectively? Further on, this subject—the meaning of the terms "involving of interests" —will be resumed, page 45, when we come to speak of adult daughters.

The first obvious defect in Mr. Mill's position, the basis of his system of *universal* exclusion against women, must strike every eye. "All," says Mr. Mill, "in the previous part of his 'Article on Government,' whose interests are not involved in those of other individuals having votes in the representation, ought themselves to have votes. But the interest of *all* children is so involved: therefore *all* children ought to be without votes." So far good logic, whatever may be thought of the philosophy or the reason of the position. But he goes on and says, "*Almost* all women find their interest involved either in that of their fathers, or in that of their husbands: therefore *all* women should be excluded from political rights."

Qu. 1.] *Universal Exclusion from partial Premises.* 29

Suppose Mr. Mill were, on some rural excursion or city perambulation, to fall into the company of a dozen smugglers or highwaymen. Suppose the philosopher and moralist were arrested with the law-breakers: suppose the judge and jury were to determine that *almost all* the thirteen had offended against a law whose penalty was transportation, and that therefore *all* the thirteen should be transported. Who would so loudly or so justly exclaim against the stupidity and barbarity of such a sentence as the unoffending author of the "Article on Government"? In vain would the judge refer him to his own philosophy contained in that celebrated "Article on Government," to his own identical logic. "*Almost all* women," says the judge, " find their interests involved in those of men: " therefore *all* women must be excluded. *Almost all*, even " all but yourself of the group with which you were found, " and all of them being of the same sex to which you " belong, are liable by law to transportation: therefore *all*, " yourself included, must pay the penalty." What could the innocent writer reply? that his philosophy, his logic, was only meant for women who could not reason, and was good enough for them? but that he was a man, and could reason, and would therefore insist on good logic from both judge and jury? that whatever might be said as to women, could not apply to him, as he was no woman but a man, demanding, there, equal justice, to be punished with others if guilty like them, but if not guilty to be discharged, though all his sex but himself had been concerned in the offence? Suppose the judge were to make a proposition to the indignant moralist, to the effect that as soon as he remodeled his logic towards the despised half of his fellow-creatures and wrote, "*almost all* women's interests "*are* involved, therefore *almost* all women shall be ex- "cluded," the judge would also decree, "almost all of "your group have committed the offence, therefore, not "all but *almost* all shall be punished;"—would the moralist submit to the degradation of having reasoned falsely, even to escape transportation?

Of this it would be hard to form an opinion: not so of the comparative injustice of the judge and the philosopher. The want of discrimination in the judge, would but occasionally punish an unfortunate moralist falling into bad company: the want of discrimination of the philosopher, would punish for a short period (before marriage) *almost* the whole of women, and for their whole lives a very considerable portion, perhaps a fourth (those without husbands or fathers), in consequence of a supposition inapplicable, on his own statement, to them.

Let us see now what proportion of women it is, which, on Mr. Mill's principles rightly applied, should enjoy political rights; their interest not being involved in that of any persons possessing political rights. Wives and daughters are the only two classes of women whose interests the "Article" involves in that of men, namely of their husbands and fathers. All women, having neither husbands nor fathers, and therefore without any one to represent their interests, stand entitled, like men, to political rights. What women stand in this predicament on the statement of the "Article"? All those not having living fathers, or having left their fathers' establishment, between the age of twenty-one and the time of their marriage; all those who never marry; all widows.

Why should all these classes of women, who by the showing of the "Article" itself have not any persons to represent them, be excluded from political rights necessary to their protection, as to that of all other human beings? For the exclusion of these women who have neither fathers nor husbands to embrace their interests, the "Article" offers no justification.

To *all* women, of *age* and *unmarried*, the law of most civilized countries awards an equality of civil rights with few exceptions, and those not caused by any notions of identity of interest, with their fathers or other persons; thus negativing the strange assumption of an identity of interest with their fathers or any other human beings.

How large a portion of the adults of the human race do the above three classes form! from one sixth perhaps to one fourth, according to the varying manners of nations leading more or less of women, and at an earlier or later age, to become wives! Yet all these are to share in the general proscription! All these whose interests are admitted *not* to be involved in those of any other human beings, are to be excluded from the political right of representation, because *other* women are said to be *virtually* represented by their husbands or fathers!

If the "Article" refuse to admit these avowedly unrepresented classes of women, what becomes of the grand argument of the "Article," for the political right to representation of all men? of the argument founded on the want of an identity of interest between the possessors of power and those subjected to it, between the makers and administrators of the laws and those who are compelled to obey them? By the *statement*, the "Article" admits a portion of women, those not having fathers or husbands,

—namely, the three classes above mentioned,—to have no more identity of interest with others than men have. By the strangest turn that ever logician made in the reasoning of so few lines, these women, not coming under his rule of identity of interest, and allowed by his term *almost* not to come under it, are to be equally excluded from the right of representation with those other women who do come under it. The statement and just reasoning from it, admit them. Palpable and self-evident false reasoning excludes them. Fortunately, however, those non-identified women, the three classes of single women above mentioned, cannot be excluded from political rights, without excluding men—to whom the philosopher has the honor to belong; and thus uprooting the whole basis of his Argument on Government.

Perhaps, however, rather than relinquish altogether the political rights of men, the author of the "Article" would even condescend to admit these non-identified classes of the degraded half of the race to a participation of those rights. " Yes, rather than that all men should be slaves, " let *some* women be free!" Should such an exclamation be extorted from his liberality or selfishness, the admission might be supported by stronger reasons than want of an identity of interest, by stronger reasons than those which could apply to any of the non-represented classes of men. There are no classes of *men* who are so much exposed to suffer wrong, who stand so much in need of the protection of political rights as these three classes of women. Disadvantages in all shapes, and on every side, surround them, in their competition with men. These disadvantages chiefly arise from four sources; from want of strength as compared with men, from want of wealth as compared with men, from want of knowledge and skill in almost every line of advancement as compared with men, and from difference of organization subjecting them to occasional losses of wealth and time, to which men are not subjected. No classes of men are liable to these tremendous, because mostly combined, evils, in their dealings and competitions with each other. If wealth be wanting to men, they have skill and strength; if strength be wanting, they have wealth and skill; if skill be wanting, they have wealth or strength, or perhaps both; and none of them are liable, as a class, to any inconveniences from organization consuming occasionally their time and wealth. If all *men* therefore, merely because no others can be found possessing political rights in whom their interests are identified, should in their own persons take care of their own interests, by contributing to name those who frame the regulations which dispose of their happiness; how much more unanswerable becomes this argument when applied to a portion, adult, sentient, and rational, of the human race, whom nature, laws, and manners, have conspired to render liable to, and defenceless under, the unmitigated wrongs of the male part of their fellow-creatures, and altogether unprepared to enter into an equal competition for the means of happiness with them? If the argument from want of sympathy, where even an equality of natural advantages prevails, (as between different portions of men,) be incontrovertible; how overpowering must it be, when to a want of sympathy is added a host of natural inequalities, and when again to these are added a still more appalling host of factitious inequalities, which the past brutality of men has heaped on these as well as other classes of women, by withholding from them equal facilities for the acquisition of knowledge and wealth?

Is it necessary further to prove, what the statement of the "Article" in fact admits, though the inference perversely denies it, that these three classes of women, not having their interests involved in that of husbands or fathers, are equally entitled to nominate representatives with men? On the admission of the "Article" their case rests: identity of interest, its only rule, does not exclude them. These three classes of women, having neither fathers nor husbands, ought, therefore, on the showing of the "Article" itself, to participate in political rights.

We pass on then to the two remaining divisions, by name excluded by the "Article," constituting perhaps the majority of adult women, viz. those who have either fathers or husbands.

The situations of the two classes of women, adult daughters and wives, though unceremoniously jumbled together along with children, by the author of the "Article," are altogether different, both as to civil rights and to privations and enjoyments. Even as to the one ruling point of identity of interest, their situations are so different as to demand separate consideration.

II. The situation of the second great division of women, of adult daughters living in their fathers' establishments, next claims our attention.

Is it true then that the interest of this class, that of adult women having living fathers, is involved in that of their fathers? A proposition more contrary to the real facts of the case, than the affirmative, was perhaps never uttered.

But there is first to be noticed the case of a considerable portion of women of this class, of whom perhaps even the "Article" would not assert that their interest is involved in that of their fathers; so contrary would such assertion be to the real facts of the case. These women, are adult *illegitimate* daughters. The fathers of illegitimate daughters have also most frequently legitimate children also. Either the illegitimate are almost entirely neglected, or between them and the legitimate springs up a competition for good offices and wealth, so that it is plainly impossible for the father to possess an identity of interest and feeling towards all these opposing claims. Instead of encouraging sympathy and identity of interest with these unfortunate children, a barbarous public opinion rather encourages alienation and desertion on the part of the parent—desertion as to every thing but the mere means of existence. In the whole treatment of women by men, such is the public opinion which men club together to form, and which they call morality, that in almost all cases where all the evil of a vice or a crime can be made to fall on the woman, and the enjoyment can be reserved for the man, such an arrangement of pain and pleasure is made. All the benefits are reserved to the stronger, the privations are thrown upon the weaker party; less able to-be-sure to bear them; but, of what avail such claim to humanity and justice, as they are at the same time less able to complain, or to make their complaints efficient? With respect to illegitimate children, particularly daughters, this hypocritical and most pernicious inequality of censure and pain is perhaps as flagrant as in any other case whatever. Disgrace and privation, by way of punishment, are inflicted on the unoffending child, who could have committed no offence, on whom therefore punishment by way of reformation or intimidation is thrown away, while in the way of example it strikes not fathers or any men capable of becoming such : on the contrary, it relieves them from the fear of punishment by throwing all its burden on the shoulders of others : punishment is inflicted on those only whom men's vicious conduct has thrown upon a world of misery. Men keeping each other in countenance, no disgrace alights on them; nor does any privation follow in the train of such disgrace. The real criminal holds up his head and smiles, if not glories, while the victim only is punished. Between these two classes of beings, it will not be pretended that much sympathy, that much identity of interest prevails, that the happiness of the one, as soon as adult, becomes involved in that of the other. And yet if this be not so, such women, so unprotected beyond all the other members of society, finding no one having a share in the representation in whose their interest is involved, ought, according to the principles of the "Article," to have themselves as direct an influence as any other members of society, in the nomination of representatives. And yet for these, perhaps the most isolated and unprotected of human beings, the most opposed to any thing like a community of interest with any other human beings, and frequently least of all with their fathers, is no sort of exception or provision made by the author of the " Article." They have the misfortune to be daughters, to belong to the proscribed half of the human race; and whether legitimate or illegitimate, they are equally shut out from political rights. Had they been sons, whether legitimate or illegitimate, as soon as they become adults, their claim to equal political rights is granted; no fiction of an identity of interest between natural sons and their fathers is sought out, no philosophical, to keep in countenance legal, fictions; the interest of illegitimate *sons* is allowed to be as distinct from that of their fathers, as those of any other men from each other: as parental authority ceases at twenty-one, so do civil and political rights and duties, as to sons, then commence.

If neither existing laws nor the philosophy of the "Article" pretend that the interest of illegitimate sons is involved in that of their fathers, with what front can so gross a fiction be urged, as that the interest of illegitimate daughters is involved in that of their fathers, though that of illegitimate sons is allowed not to be so involved? Neither the one nor the other is any way necessarily involved, but rather the reverse; and least of all that of the daughters

Here then we find rescued from the ban of political proscription another mass of women besides the three classes first mentioned, from want of an identity of interest with any of those exercising political rights. This mass must be deducted from the division of adult daughters. It is now time to examine the pretext on which the "Article" affirms that legitimate adult daughters, having living fathers, ought to be excluded from political rights.

First, "the interest of adult daughters is no more in-"volved than that of adult sons in the interest of their "fathers." As soon as sons arrive at the age of manhood, the "Article" admits that their interest ceases to be involved in that of their fathers. If therefore the sympathies of fathers, as proved by their ordinary conduct, cannot be shown to be *more* strong in favor of their daughters than of their sons, so much more strong as that the interest of the one shall be in all essential matters undistinguishable from that of the other, no ground can, on that account, be shown for the exclusion of adult daughters from political any more than from civil rights, which would not equally apply to the sons. This—whether fathers sympathize more strongly with their daughters than their sons—is a question of fact, which may be safely referred to the individual experience of every one.

One obvious feature in this comparison is, that the organization and occupation, the pleasures and pursuits, of the sons being the same as, or analogous to, those of the fathers, more sympathy is necessarily excited on the part of the fathers towards the sons than to the daughters. From all that are called, by a very ordinary mixture of brutality and hypocrisy, *manly* pleasures, daughters are excluded; excluded not only from participation in, but from allusion to, them. As to all the pleasures of the senses, reserve and restraint are the rules invariably enforced towards the daughters; while licence and unbounded gratification, limited only by prudence as to pecuniary means, are the prerogatives liberally conceded to the sons. If the fathers, from exhaustion or disease, are no longer able to indulge in the short-lived gratifications of sensual excess, they can talk over and bring back into life the memory of their faded joys, and live them over again in association with their sons' existing enjoyments. Of these, reserved for the nobler half of the race, the ignoble, the ignorant, (the innocent) part, the daughters, must not hear the names named. With the little pleasures of the daughters, the colours and fashion of their clothes and such matters, which are left to such creatures as, suited to their amiable imbecility, their lordly superiors do not deign, or but rarely and through condescension, to hold communion: to such insipidities their manly nerves are not attuned.

If from the associations of enjoyments founded on a similarity of organization and circumstances, we turn to the pursuits of life, we find the same similarity engendering sympathy between the sons and the fathers, the same dissimilarity between the pursuits of the daughters and the fathers. Business, professions, political concerns, local affairs, the whole field of sciences and arts, are open to the united and mutually sympathizing efforts of the males. To their mutual judgments and speculations, the disposal of the family income and capital are intrusted. From all these commanding sources of intellectual and muscular activity, the daughters, like the little children, are excluded, previous care having been taken, by shutting them out from all means of intellectual culture, and from the view of and participation in the real incidents of active life, to render them as unfit for, as unambitious of, such high occupations. Confined, like other domestic animals, to the house and its little details, their "sober wishes" are never permitted "to stray" into the enlarged plains of general speculation and action. The dull routine of domestic incidents is the world to them, except when an occasional vista opens upon the actors in real life, through the long aisles of superstition, or the unsubstantial glitter of meretricious public amusements. All the numerous marts for mingled recreation, information, and discussion, on politics, trade, and literature, or all but the most insignificant, such as those which merely excite the feelings but afford no scope for the judgment, are shut to daughters, while to adult sons they are as open as to fathers, and afford them a theatre for an ever-renewing interchange of emotion and interest. Sons are most frequently embarked in the very same business with their fathers: the judgments of both are exercised on the same interesting propositions: success or failure are equally participated, not only as to pecuniary consequences, but as to mental effort and the anxieties of the pursuit. In all these things opposed to the pursuits of the sons, do the pursuits of daughters stand. With their blank of life and of active pursuit, how can the active father sympathize? The interest of the sons may be at times mistaken by fathers for their own, and may seem to be involved in it; the interest of daughters, except from peculiarity of circumstances, never. Yet no one has been ingenuous enough to propose, much less to justify, the exclusion of sons from political rights in consequence of a real similarity in the sympathies and frequently in the interests of their fathers with them; but in the case of daughters, though no such similarity in the sympathies or interests exists, it is quite enough to *feign* an identity, and to jump over fact and inference, to the exclusion of adult daughters for the unpardonable offence, in the eye of Mr. Mill's new, as well as of the old political philosophy, of being on an average about four or five inches shorter in stature than the sons!

So much more completely is the interest of the sons involved than that of the daughters in the interest of fathers, that as soon as the daughters become adult, they, necessarily operated upon by the system under which they live, look out of their artificial cages of restraint and imbecility, to catch glances at the world with the hope of freedom from parental control, by leaving behind them the very name of their fathers, and vainly hoping for happiness without independence, in the gratification of one passion,

Qu. 1.] *Adult Daughters seek new Name and Connexions.* 41

love, round which their absurd training for blind male sensuality, has caused all their little anxieties to centre. The adult sons go in and out of the father's house when they choose: they are frequently treated with liberality as visitors or equals. But the adult daughters are, for the most part, under as much restraint as little children: they must ask leave to open the door or take a walk: not one of their actions that does not depend on the will of another: they are never permitted, like the sons, to regulate their conduct by their own notions of propriety and prudence and to restrain them where necessary, like rational beings, from a regard to their consequences: every thing is prescribed to them: their reason and foresight are not cultivated like those of the sons; and the despotism which creates their imbecility, adduces its own work as a justification of its unrelenting pressure and of its eternal duration. To marriage therefore, as the only means allowed them of emerging from paternal control; as the only means of gratifying one passion, to which all their thoughts have been exclusively directed, but which they are at the same time told it is highly improper they should wish to enjoy; as the only means of obtaining, through cunning and blandishment, that direction of their own voluntary actions, which all rational beings ought to possess, and which is the sure and only basis of intelligence and morals; to marriage, as the fancied haven of pleasure and freedom—the freedom of the slave to-be-sure, to be acquired not by right but by coaxing, by the influence of passions inapplicable to the cold despotism of the fathers —daughters look forward. No sooner adult, than their home and their name are daughters anxious to get rid of, because the retaining of them is made incompatible with the only views of happiness presented to them. Almost equally anxious with the daughters are the fathers to encourage this propensity, It is the interest of the fathers, the vulgar, palpable, *apparent* interest here in view, and every where in Mr. Mill's " Article," not the remote comprehensive interest of enlightened benevolence, to *dispose* of their daughters as quickly and on as good terms—with as small a portion—as possible; to give them up as breeding stock into the hands of some man, to whom the laws, made by men, every where give the faculty of thinking for them and prescribing all their actions, without any regard to their volitions, further than good policy for their own ease, or caprice, may suggest. " Better to be a slave and be kissed, than to be a slave without kissing." Such is the alternative for adult daughters!—the slaves of husbands by law, the slaves of fathers, in spite of a vain law, by the imbecilities induced by education and circumstances, by dependence on the fathers' bounty for existence, and by an unrelenting public opinion—the manufacture, and watch-word, of their despots.

Yet, says the grave author of the " Article on Government," *the interest of daughters is involved in that of their fathers!* In one respect indeed the palpable, apparent, interest of adult daughters is involved in that of their fathers, namely in parting as soon as possible; in the same sense that the interest of a husband and wife who hate each other is involved in bringing about a less amicable separation.

Had the "Article" asserted that the interest of adult daughters was involved in that of their *Mothers*, there would have been some appearance of truth, some plausibility in the statement; but for a philosopher so far to rely on the stupifying effects of the habitual exercise of despotism on the minds of the male creatures whom he addressed, as to ask their assent to a proposition, as palpably false as would be the assertion that adult daughters had neither eyes, ears, tastes, feelings, or passions, or any wish for enjoyment, any delight in guiding their own actions free from external control, is indeed a wonderful exemplification of the force of habit in blinding, not only the judgment, but the power of observing facts of daily and hourly occurrence. The adult daughter is kept, by the master of the family, under the same system of restraint as to voluntary action, the same system of privation as to enjoyment, as the mother; from all which restraints on freedom of action and of enjoyment—of course liable always to the law and to their own calculations as to the consequences of their actions—the adult sons are freed. The restraints on adult daughters it is true are not, like those of the mothers, imposed by law, but simply those of education, custom and public opinion, engendering such a moral and physical persecution in case of disobedience as renders the vain permission of law a dead letter. Had a positive law sanctioned these restraints on adult daughters, we should be told that this law was the preserver, *for their own happiness,* of the morals of daughters, and similar disgusting and insulting hypocrisy, and that the abolition of such laws would open the floodgates to licentiousness and every species of vice. Yet, without any laws on the subject, we do, in point of fact, find that the power of restraint of fathers is as efficient over adult daughters as over wives.—This will be resumed when we speak of the law-supported, literally existing slavery of wives. Liable to the same privations and restraints then, doomed to fulfil the same subordinate offices in life, educated to the same unhealthy sensibility, uncomprehensiveness, and general destitution of mind, mothers must look upon, must feel the interests of their daughters as being much more nearly involved in their interest, than fathers can feel them. The mother, shut out for the most part, like any other upper servant, not only from the management but from the knowledge of the family's, that is to say, of the father's, property, is sensible of no loss in providing liberally for the daughters, and feels none of those opposing views and interests, which more comprehensive, if not more benevolent, views are apt to produce in the father. The mother, proverbially, is always wishing to procure enjoyments, *stolen pleasures,* for her children (and daughters are while they live treated as children); the pecuniary means of procuring which, mostly innocent, domestic pleasures, are frequently absorbed in the external tumultuous dissipations of the adult males of the family.

Is it not then plain that the palpable apparent interest of the daughters, is much more likely to be considered by the mothers, than by the fathers, to be involved in theirs? Is it not in point of truth and fact much more intimately involved? But according to the principles of the " Article," every adult person, whose interest is not involved in that of some other person whose interest is represented, ought to have a direct voice in the representation. But the interest of the daughters being more involved in that of the mothers than of any other individual, the question, according to Mr. Mill's reasoning, is, have these mothers a vote? have they political rights? The reply being necessarily in the negative, the consequence is that adult daughters are as fully entitled, in order to promote their own personal happiness as members of a community of human beings, to a vote in the representation and to other political rights, as adult sons can, for the same simple and unanswerable reason, be.

Even by the civil and criminal laws of all countries, advanced ever so little beyond barbarism, is a flat contradiction given to this assumption of an identity, or involving, of interests between adult daughters and their fathers. Daughters of legal age have generally the same nominal legal protection from the personal violence and restraints of fathers, that sons of the same age enjoy: and this protection is the same or nearly the same against fathers as against any other individuals. Any property also they may acquire, by gifts or otherwise, belongs to themselves, and can no more be directly invaded by the fathers than by any other persons. Though it be true that the indirect influence of fathers over their daughters, resulting from habits acquired in education, from the possession of knowledge and wealth, and from public opinion, reduces these nominal legal protections to little more than abstract points of philosophy as to the real independence of daughters, yet the very existence of such legal protection is an admission of evils to be guarded against, of the universal inclination of those possessing power without checks, fathers or others, to use that power for their own exclusive interest, though not quite to the extent of reducing those subjected to it to a state of destitution equal to that of the slaves in the West Indies.

A cloud of obscurity is wont to be thrown over this question of identity, or involving, of interests. No expression is more general or vague, or liable to a greater variety of meanings. So much the better is it adapted to the purposes of sophistry and oppression. There is an identity of interest between all human beings of all nations, were they enlightened enough, in spite of the prejudices of education and pernicious institutions moulding their actions and minds, to perceive it. There is an identity of interest, less confined and less difficult to ordinary comprehension, between all the members, though amounting to many millions, male and female, of the same political community. There is a still stronger and plainer identity of interest between those of the same province or town, from circumstances increasing in number as the circle lessens, affecting the well-being of each individual within such circle. A still stronger and more palpable identity of interest prevails between the members of the same family, as separated from every other family by its individual stock of wealth, the result of the combined exertions of the family, resting on the common feeling of a still increased number of pleasures and pains. But even this identity of interest, in the ordinary, apparent, acceptation of the term, extends but to the mere surface of the causes which operate on individual happiness. It is the *general* interest of the family, as it is of the town, the province, the nation, the universe, that as great a quantity of the articles of wealth and all other means of happiness as possible should be attainable by the whole universe, nation, province, town, and family, respectively. But this general interest attained, a second question springs up as to the *distribution* of these means of happiness. Each nation, each province, each town, each family, wishes to obtain as large a share as possible of all these means of happiness. But does the tendency to division of interests stop here? By no means. It must proceed, and ought to proceed, until it is brought home to every *individual* of every family. There is no such thing as a general, abstract, happiness. All happiness is made up of that of individuals. To delude individuals from their just claim to personal happiness, politicians, priests, and statesmen, have played off many fraudulent expressions, as the interest of the state, of the church, of the national glory, of the national wealth, &c., meaning always their own individual interest. Within the bosom of the individuals of families this individual interest dwells: there it must be sought out and individually promoted. Let wealth and all other means of happiness exist in ever such profusion in a family as in a nation, little is done as to happiness, until these *means* are rightly *distributed*. If an equal share of these do not fall to every individual according to wants and capabilities of enjoyment, an equal share of all the means of happiness, and more particularly and above all, an equal share of the power of *self-government*, an ingredient without which neither intelligence, morality, nor happiness, can exist, the absolute mass of the means of happiness is not in the remotest degree an index to the absolute quantum of happiness enjoyed by that family. It is impossible that the happiness of any individual should be, strictly speaking, involved in that of another, from dissimilarity of constitution, from moral and physical causes, more particularly where the organization in some respects differs. Shades of variety of views and tastes, must occasionally prevail. But even if these dissimilarities did not exist, the very act of placing the means of happiness or the command of the actions of the one in dependence on the pleasure of the other, would break the charm and destroy this identity of interest. Strong affection or improved reason may, where perfect equality prevails, lead to an identification of interest: for *power* not being invested in such case, in the hands of either over the other, mutual respect and persuasion must be resorted to, to induce harmony of will. But the moment that power is given to either, it is an absolute contradiction in terms to speak of identity of interest; for if the identity existed, there would be no need of power to enforce obedience. To produce a real identity of interest between any two individuals; first, all power to injure or molest must be taken away equally from both; next, benevolence and reason must have been so comprehensively cultivated by both, that they shall both perceive that it is their mutual interest to promote in every thing the real happiness of each other. If the "Article" will gravely maintain that such a state of things exists between adult daughters and fathers in any part of the world, it may still continue, in its next edition, the astounding assertion that the interest of daughters is involved in that of their fathers.

The gross, the vague interest, because it is the only one that exists, in which there is any thing analogous to an identity of interest, as alluded to by the "Article," between the daughters and the father, must be that which depends on the increasing or decreasing wealth of the master of the family and owner of all the wealth, to be distributed in whatever manner that master thinks fit, amongst its members. Whatever may be the absolute inequality of the shares of wealth and other means of happiness, dealt out to the different members of the family, the share of each, however absolutely dissimilar, would most probably be increased by the abundance and good-nature which prosperous circumstances are wont to produce, and would be apt to be lessened by the opposite circumstances arising from ill-success. In other words, the *treatment* of the individual members of the family,—sons, daughters, breeding-women, servants, slaves, and all other denominations of sentient beings,—may be improved by the prosperity of the affairs of the master, or deteriorated by his reverses or change of character. But what has this to do with individual identity of interest, with an equality of happiness necessarily co-existing between two individuals, so that in promoting the one, that of the other should be promoted *in an equal degree,* not added to in its particular sphere of *unequal enjoyment,* like the comforts of horses, dogs, or poultry?

All the members of a family, like all the members of a community, have a common interest as against all the world beside : but as the members of a community have also particular interests as to each other, so have the members of families all of them their own particular and individual interests. The ox is better fed when the master is rich : so far the common interest extends :—but wherefore? because it is the interest of the master that the ox should be fattened as speedily as possible in order to be consumed. The *permanent* interest of the ox, that of health and long life, is sacrificed : his immediate pleasure of eating is promoted, because it coincides with the interest of the owner. No comfort is given to the ox but with subserviency to this superior claim of the master's interest. So with respect to all other beings—servants, daughters, sons, &c., in his power. The interest of each of them, is promoted, in as far only as it is coincident with, or subservient to, the master's interest. The more intelligent doubtless, particularly if at the same time benevolent, the master, father or not father, may be, the more numerous the points of coincidence he will discover between his interest and that of his dependents, though his power be unrestrained. Unrestrained power is however the surest method of destroying this intelligence and benevolence. The interests of adult sons, then, coinciding more nearly with those of the masters, their fathers, are more promoted by the fathers: though even here, how soon does the pursuit of individual wealth falsify the notion of an involving of interests! Then come the interests of the daughters, coinciding in comparatively few points with that of the fathers. Next the servants, between whom and the masters still fewer points of coincidence present themselves : and last of all, the domestic animals. As many sources of enjoyment as are open to the master, so many are all the rational adult members of the family capable of desiring, the pleasure of freedom from constraint being not the least conspicuous. But if the master's wealth be not capable of gratifying these desires, and his benevolence boundless, there must be a contrariety of interest between the different individual members, extending to every ungratified desire. The involving or identity of interest, is only then the *exception*, occurring when two interests happen to coincide: contrariety of interest is the general rule. And the mere power of law, that is, force in the ultimate resort, supported by superstition and opinion, is the rude means of compressing clashing interests, and preventing those eternal open collisions which they would seem calculated to produce. Because the slave or servant of necessity submits to the established order, the order established universally by the masters, it does not follow that the interests, the pleasures and pains, of the servant or the slave, are involved in those of the master.

Can any thing therefore be more shallow or pitiful, more unworthy the name of common sense, not to speak of philosophy, than the pretence that the interest of daughters is, not only involved in that of fathers; but so differently and superiorly involved, so much beyond the interest of any other branches of the family, as to justify a particular exclusion of the daughters from political rights, in consequence of that identity?

Were any further aid wanting to show the futility of the notion of any peculiar identity of interest between daughters and fathers, we should find it in the laws themselves which exclude them from political rights; which in most civilized countries liberate the daughters as well as the sons from parental control as soon as they become adult. The father has no more *legal* power to constrain the actions of the adult daughters than of the adult sons: nor does his legal power over either sons or daughters extend further than that of any other individual over them. 'Tis true that the father possesses a great moral power over both sons and daughters, from the associations of education and intercourse, from the command of their present means of existence, and from the exclusive possession of the family wealth, necessary to establish both daughters and sons in life. Daughters are as much amenable to the laws, and can enter into contracts as freely as sons: but education and opinion render these equal civil rights of law utterly useless to the daughters, while liberty of acting and pecuniary means of independent action, being frequently given by the fathers to the sons, they are enabled to avail themselves of their legal civil rights. Now if the law contemplated that there was any such thing as an identity of interest between daughters and fathers, so as to cause the one to be involved in that of the other, how superfluous this power given to adult daughters to oppose the will of their fathers, as often, and just in the same manner as to the sons, as their calculations of interest might render it in their minds prudent to exercise such opposition. The law gives the lie to the vain pretence of an identity of interest. If the interests were identified, why not leave to the fathers the making of civil contracts for the daughters though adult? why not make the father answerable for expenses and extravagancies of adult daughters, nay answerable to the penalties of the laws for the daughters' breach of them? None of these things are done as respects adult daughters more than as respects adult sons. An incompatibility of interest with their fathers, is by the law admitted to be as probable on the part of daughters as of sons; even laws recognise a *contrariety;* and therefore liberty is reserved to adult daughters, as fully as to the sons, of refusing obedience to fathers, when exacted in opposition to their real or apparent interest. Here then is provision made by law for a contrariety of interest in all the ordinary transactions of every-day life between daughters and fathers, just as between sons and fathers. But while this contrariety of interest is admitted by law to exist in the detail, it is denied in the gross by philosophy; and on so monstrous a fiction is founded the exclusion of daughters from political rights, the indispensable basis, not only admitted but maintained by the "Article," for the secure and continued enjoyment of civil rights and individual happiness.

As far then as regards *one* of the two classes of women, whose interests the "Article" asserts to be involved in that of men, as far as respects the interests of *daughters*; it has been shown that from the totally different objects and oc-

Qu. 1.] *Summary respecting State of Adult Daughters.* 53

cupations in life, difference of pleasures pains and privations, difference of views for the future, between adult daughters and fathers, nothing can be more gratuitous and contrary to every day's experience, than to assert that the interest of the one is involved in that of the other. It has been shown that though the interest of adult sons, as every day experience also proves, is much more involved in that of their fathers than that of adult daughters, yet are not political rights withheld from the sons while the fathers live, in consequence of this pretended identity. It has been shown that the interest of adult daughters is, in point of fact, from circumstances obvious and easy to be explained, much more involved in that of their mothers, who are equally deprived with them of a voice in the representation, than in that of their fathers. It has been shown that even the laws, in England, acknowledge and provide for a contrariety of interest between adult daughters and fathers, by depriving the latter of all direct legal control over the actions of the daughters; the command of wealth, education, male-created and male-supported public opinion, being the sources of that more rigid despotism than that over the sons, to which necessity compels daughters to submit, their minds for the most part as well as their bodies being fashioned to the yoke. It has been also shown, that the vague and popular sense in which the interest of the daughters can be said to be involved in that of the fathers, applies as much to the sons and to all members of the family, rational or irrational, in their several scales of enjoyment, as to adult daughters; that it amounts to no more than a probability of better treatment under prosperous, and a worse under decaying circumstances, the character of the head of the family remaining the same.

III. Of the situation of the last great division of women, Wives.

The next division of women, *wives*, and by far the most numerous and therefore the most important, whose interest the "Article" asserts to be involved in that of some assignable *males*, namely their husbands, having, or who ought to have, votes in the representation, next demands our attention. This very numerous portion of the human race, the " Article" asserts, ought to be debarred from political rights, because their husbands, in whose interests theirs are said to be involved and identified, possess, or ought to possess, such rights.

Man, uninstructed, unknowing the pleasures of sympathy, has every where sought to render his fellow-beings, as well as brutes and the inanimate powers of nature, subservient to his immediate gratification; and by the same means—those of universal force, aided by superior skill and cunning. The strong and knowing, without checks on their conduct, have every where reduced the great mass of their fellows, either to a state of absolute slavery, or more or less partaking of the attributes of that state. But of all their fellows, those whom they could most easily subjugate, as being deficient in strength stature and bulk, were the class of women, parcelled out amongst men, from the necessity of sexual delights to each of their masters, one weak always coupled and subjected to one strong,—the minds and habits of women moulded to the supposed barbarous interests of their short-sighted keepers: what wonder that women have been made to obey the general law of subjection to force, and have hitherto submitted to be considered *blanks* in the creation, entitled to no physical, intellectual, or sympathetic, enjoyments, on their own account, and *for their own sakes*, but simply as rendering them more useful instruments, more stimulating provocatives, to the ignorant selfish propensities of men? Had the constitution of things been such that man was independent of women for the gratification of his most imperious passion, that he had no sexual desires, and that women perpetuated the race without his intervention, or at least without his intervention in the way of pleasure; we should have seen women, because weaker, converted every where by the law of force, into field and manufacturing laborers for the exclusive benefit of the males. How far, and in what way, the necessary instrumentality of women to men's sexual enjoyments, modifies, and but modifies, the destiny of women, (their universal degradation, privation of equal improvement and equal enjoyment,) for the unpardonable vice of inferior physical strength, we shall presently perceive. If the domination of man be from this cause, with a view to the increase of his own pleasures, modified over women in general; what has been his conduct towards that numerous class of this branch of his fellow-beings, whom he condescends to honor with the name of *wives?*

By way of distinguishing and honoring this class of the proscribed half of the human race, man condescends to enter into what he calls a *contract* with certain women, for certain purposes, the most important of which is, the producing and rearing of children to maturity. Each man yokes a woman to his establishment, and calls it a *contract.* Audacious falsehood! A contract! where are any of the attributes of contracts, of equal and just contracts, to be found in this transaction? A contract implies the voluntary assent of both the contracting parties. Can even both the parties, man and woman, by agreement alter the terms, as to *indissolubility* and *inequality,* of this pretended contract? No. Can any individual man divest himself, were he even so inclined, of his power of despotic control? He cannot. Have women been consulted as to the terms of this pretended contract? A contract, all of whose enjoyments—wherever nature has not imposed a physical bar on the depravity of selfishness—are on one side, while all of its pains and privations are on the other! A contract, giving all power, arbitrary will and unbridled enjoyment to the one side; to the other, unqualified obedience, and enjoyments meted out or withheld at the caprice of the ruling and enjoying party. Such a contract, as the owners of *slaves* in the West Indies and every other slave-polluted soil, enter into with their slaves— the law of the stronger imposed on the weaker, *in contempt* of the interests and wishes of the weaker. As little as slaves have had to do in any part of the world in the enacting of slave-codes, have women in any part of the world had to do with the partial codes of selfishness and ignorance, which every where dispose of their right over their own actions and all their other enjoyments, in favor of those who made the regulations; particularly that most unequal and debasing code, absurdly called the *contract* of marriage. This, alas! the best boon that the selfishness and ignorance of men have permitted them to grant to women—compelling at least the waywardness of man to provide, till adult age, for the children he begat—this pretended contract is, as to the women, in every other respect the law of restraint and exclusion, the law of the stronger, enacted with reference to the enjoyments of that stronger alone; and no more consulting the interests of women, the other pretended contracting party, than the interests of bullocks are consulted in the police regulations that precede and follow their slaughter. From regulating the terms of this pretended contract, women have been as completely excluded as bullocks, or sheep, or any other animals subjugated to man, have been from determining the regulations of commons or slaughter-houses. Men enacted, that is to say, *willed* the terms, let women like them or not: man to be the owner, master, and ruler of every thing, even to the minutest action, and most trifling article of property brought into the common stock by the woman; woman to be the moveable property, and ever-obedient servant, to the bidding of man.

"But women may or may not marry! they may refuse " to enter into this contract." So when, in happier times of East India monopoly, the food of provinces was bought up by individuals under the shield of mercantile political power, the poor people were kindly told, "they were at " liberty to buy or not to buy." But if they did not buy, the trifling inconvenience of the alternative was, that they must starve. So by male-created laws, depriving women of knowledge and skill, excluding them from the benefit of all judgment and mind-creating offices and trusts, cutting them off almost entirely from the participation, by succession or otherwise, of property, and from its uses and exchanges—are women kindly told, " they are " free to marry or not." Things are so arranged, knowledge, property, civil as well as political exclusions, man's public opinion, that the great majority of adult women must marry on whatever terms their masters have willed, or starve: or if not absolutely starve, they must renounce at least all the means of enjoyment monopolized by the males. Under these circumstances, man makes it a condition, under which he admits women into a participation—always limited however by his uncontrolled will—of his means of happiness dependent on wealth, that woman shall, like the negro-slave, surrender to him all control over her actions, except where those actions are regulated by the higher penalties of the law, to all of which she is equally exposed, to many with more severity, than man.

But, says the "Article on Government," the interest of wives is involved in that of their husbands; and their husbands having, or it being just that they should have, votes in the representation which enacts the laws by which their actions and happiness are controlled, it is superfluous that women should have second votes, all their interests being already *virtually* represented and provided for by means of their husbands' votes.

We have already seen, in the case of adult daughters, that the law itself disallows the pretext of an identity of interest between daughters and fathers, by taking away from the father all *direct* control over the actions of daughters to the same extent as over those of sons. From the time of adolescence up to the time of marriage, the law of England supposes a perfect capacity on the part of the adult woman as well as of the adult man, whether the father be alive or not, for the performance of civil obligations and for the independent guidance of moral conduct by motives of prudence and benevolence. The duration of this period of full capacity for self-government by women, liable only like men (political rights excepted, as from the immense majority of men they are now almost every where unjustly withheld) to the common laws of the and in which they live, may last for any period, some-

Qu. 1.] *government, granted to Adult Daughters.* 59

times to the whole extent of their lives, on an average perhaps, in this country, for five or six years. During all this period, the law supposes young women to be as capable as young men, of self-government, by taking all *direct* power over their actions out of the hands of all persons, and by rendering them amenable for the breach of every law, just like men. During this time, young women must be acquiring experience in the art of self-government, just like young men; and they certainly cannot become the less fit for the guidance of their own actions, the longer this experience: they must become, on the contrary, the more fit. But as soon as adult daughters become wives, their civil rights disappear; they fall back again, and remain all their lives—should their owners and directors live so long—into the state of children or idiots, the passive property of their owners; protected by the law in some few respects only, like other slaves, from the excessive abuse of despotic power. What is this mysterious circumstance in the connexion of marriage, which alters so completely the nature and interests of woman as an individual, rational, and sentient being; while it not only leaves the individual nature and interests of man untouched, but expands them, as it were, by merging in his interests those of another being equally capable of individual feelings and wishes with himself? The individual feelings and wishes of the adult daughter are not merged in those of the father: the law disclaims it. Change the father into husband, and all individual wishes and interests cease, and whatever is pleasing to the husband becomes necessarily equally pleasing to the wife; so that two volitions become superfluous to two beings so circumstanced. Perhaps it would puzzle an impartial spectator, some-one being not exactly of the same race with the human, to determine to which of those two beings, male or female, thus living together with the ostensible object of increasing each other's happiness and providing for their offspring, the exercise of the one will should be given—whether to the weaker or the stronger, to the one that could most or that could least abuse the power; or whether it ought not to be wielded alternately by each of the parties with feelings and wishes so mysteriously amalgamated.

Leaving to such being—not human—the solution of this enigma, it is worth while to look a little closely into this so mysteriously operating connexion in marriage, which unindividualizes the nature and interests of one of the parties, and operates the miracle, the moral miracle, of the philosophy of utility of the nineteenth century—of reducing two identities into one. In marriage, it will perhaps be said—for we are really anxious to penetrate the remotest, most delicate, things approaching to reasons on so mysterious a subject—man becomes dependent for one of the most copious sources of his happiness, that arising from sexual endearments, on his wife, and is therefore compelled to a kindly use of whatever despotic powers law may give him, in order to procure from woman those gratifications, the zest of which depends on the kindly inclinations of the party yielding them.

Were women utterly destitute of those feelings which render man dependent on them for their gratification; were sensibility no part of their organization, instead of being, as it now is, preposterously over-excited; were they cold as stones to feeling and to love; or had they self-control and magnanimity enough to obey the invitation of the celebrated Grecian, Aspasia, to repress their own feelings, and make their power of gratifying the imperious propensities of men, their masters, subservient to the acquiring of an equality of rights and enjoyments with their masters;—then, and in either of these cases, would there be some force in the observation, that the dependence of man for sexual enjoyment on woman necessitated a kindly use of the despotic power he usurped over her when living with her for the rearing of a family. But such is not the constitution of the human frame, such is not the constitution of woman; such is not her power of command over her feelings; such is not her comprehensiveness of mind, stunted by disuse and want of education. *Woman is more the slave of man for the gratification of her desires, than man is of woman.* To man, unmarried and speculating on marriage, by the permission of law and of public opinion, the gratification of every sexual desire is permitted, limited only by prudential considerations as to money and health, and with some few by considerations as to the effects of their actions on the happiness of those connected with them; while to woman speculating on marriage, though no law controls, yet public opinion— fruit of the selfish conspiracy of men—and *power to oppress,* arising from command of wealth and all other means of influence, being omnipotent over her, the gratification to her of these same desires is altogether prohibited. To man married, for breach of the vain and insulting promise of fidelity to his wife, no penalty is awarded by law; while public opinion extenuates the venial offence, or rather encourages and smiles upon it: while to woman married, the breach of the compulsory vow of slavish obedience, is punished at command of the husband, even by aid of the civil power; and the vow of fidelity—no empty vow to her—is enforced by the united ruin and degradation of law and public opinion, both created by man for his exclusive benefit, and unrelentingly enforced.

The despotism of man over woman in marriage, by personal force maintained, as by law established, is then rendered gentle by the dependence of man on woman for the gratification of his amorous propensities! How long shall such insulting falsehoods be substituted for reasons on which depend the happiness of one half the human race? The dependence of man on the smiles of woman, is always *voluntary* on the part of the man, and is limited to the short-lived moment previous to possession. The dependence of woman on the smiles of man is eternal, may be voluntary for a moment before the *contract*, but is unrelentingly *forced* during the whole remainder of life. Were the dependence for personal enjoyments equal, the despotic power of man in marriage would gain as much accession of force by the dependence on him of woman, as it would lose by his mutual dependence on her, and domination would be exercised just as if no such passion or dependence on either side existed. But as things are, the real dependence being by the united operation of both law and opinion, on the side of woman, sexual desires increase tenfold the facility of exercising, and of continuing for life, the despotism of men in marriage, instead of mitigating its pressure, on the slaves subjected to its ungenerous, its all-corrupting, and mutually-degrading code.

But this is not all: another and more glaring falsehood is assumed and reasoned on as fact, in the pretext of modifying man's despotism in marriage by his sexual dependence on woman. Not only is a *natural* dependence for the gratification of man's love in marriage assumed, but a legal dependence, a legal obligation, is feigned. A legal, is added to the natural, sexual dependence! It is assumed that the laws bind men to the gratification of the wives whom they take. The laws made by man, absolve him from all such dependence. Against absolute desertion, starvation, or violence threatening life, alone, the laws protect women in marriage: just as the West-India and United States Slave-codes guarantee the slaves. Such is man's dependence! Woman can demand no enjoyment from man as a matter of right: she must beg it, like any of her children, or like any slave, as a favor. If refused, she must submit, contented or not contented. Once married, a woman must submit to the *commands* of her master. Superstition is called in to the aid of despotism, and at the altar woman is constrained to devote herself a victim to the gratification of all the pleasures and legal commands (extending to all actions not erected by the law into crimes) of her owner, renouncing the voluntary direction of her own actions in favor of the man who has admitted her to the high honor of becoming his involuntary breeding machine and household slave. What then becomes of the pretended dependence of man on the voluntary compliance of woman in marriage with any of his inclinations? If woman do not comply with his caprices, man is justified by vile law and viler opinion, to compel obedience. If man refuse any request of woman, the legal, the moral, and the physical power of compelling obedience are equally wanting. Man disdains to beg for what he can command. Such voluntary compliance, the gracious result of the understanding and the affections, improving and exalting the happiness equally of the giver and receiver, is spurned by the ignorant, short-sighted, selfishness of man. He must be obeyed: and for the execrable pleasure of commanding, he loses,—and were he alone concerned, justly loses,—the delights of the sweetest human social intercourse, that of esteem and confidence between equals, heightened by the glow of sexual attachment. Man, by law, superstition, and opinion, commands: woman, in marriage, by law, superstition, and opinion, obeys. The happiness of both is sacrificed. Not only does woman obey; the despotism of man demands another sacrifice. Woman must cast nature, or feign to cast it, from her breast. She is not permitted to appear to feel, or desire. The whole of what is called her education training her to be the obedient instrument of man's sensual gratification, she is not permitted even to wish for any gratification for herself. She must have no desires: she must always yield, must submit as a matter of duty, not repose upon her equal for the sake of happiness: she must blush to own that she joys in his generous caresses, were such by chance ever given. This engrafted duplicity of character still further increases, and to an incalculable extent, the dependence of woman in marriage on man; his slave for what nature has implanted as the most innocent and useful of human desires, when not gratified at the expense of ulterior mischief or of any fellow-creature's happiness; doubly his slave, from the necessity of concealing these natural desires, and from the heartless insult with which the brutal male sensualist is wont to repress the gentlest, the humblest, the most kindly overflowings of them.

But if, from the balance of mere sexual feelings, the dependence of woman on the pernicious despotism of man, is increased instead of being mitigated, how deplorable is and must be her situation every where, when we consider that wealth and knowledge are reserved exclusively for the male as additional stays of despotism! Not satisfied with superiority of strength, man makes it but the basis on which to erect his system of sexual exclusions to gratify his unhallowed lust of domination. To secure what seem to his ignorance the advantages of superiority of strength, he makes the mind of his victim as feeble as nature, but particularly as artificial circumstances, have rendered her body, by excluding from her, and reserving to himself, all sources of knowledge and skill; by vesting in himself all power to create, all right to possess and control, property; by excluding her from all those offices, actions, and incidents, which afford opportunities for exercising the judgement, and calling into life all the higher and more useful intellectual powers; and lastly, by making her swear, when about to enter on life and assist in producing and rearing a family, to renounce the exercise of that reason of which his vile practices have deprived her, to surrender the control over her voluntary actions, to be in all things, going out and coming in, in the minutest incidents of life, *obedient* to his will, be it wise or capricious. Black slaves are not insulted with the requisition to swear or vow obedience to their masters: the compulsion of the slave-code is sufficient without unnecessary childish insult. For white slaves—parcelled out amongst men (as if to compensate them for their own cowardly submission almost every where to the chains of political power), the uninquiring instruments first of their voluptuousness, and, when that is sated, of their caprice of command—was and is reserved this gratuitous degradation of swearing to be slaves, of kissing the rod of domestic despotism, and of devoting themselves to its worship. Was it not enough to deprive women, by the iniquitous inequality of the marriage, or white-slave, code, of all the attributes of personal liberty? to invest in the hands of another human being all the attributes of despotism backed by the possession of wealth, knowledge, and strength, without the cruel mockery of exacting from her trained obsequiousness the semblance of a *voluntary* obedience, of devotedness to her degradation? What need of this heartless insult? Are not the laws, supported first by the individual strength of every individual man despotic in his own right, and next supported by the united strength of all men, sufficient to control, to compel submission from, this helpless creature? Would not the pleasure of commanding the actions and the body be complete, without the luxury and banquet of despotism, of laying prostrate the mind? would not the simple pleasure of commanding be sufficient, without the gratification of the additional power of taunting the victim with her pretended *voluntary* surrender of the control over her own actions?

Woman is then compelled, in marriage, by the possession of superior strength on the part of men, by the want of knowledge, skill and wealth, by the positive, cruel, partial, and cowardly enactments of law, by the terrors of superstition, by the mockery of a pretended vow of obedience, and to crown all, and as the result of all, by the force of an unrelenting, unreasoning, unfeeling, public opinion, to be the literal unequivocal *slave* of the man who may be styled her husband. I say emphatically the slave; for a slave is a person whose actions and earnings, instead of being, under his own control, liable only to equal laws, to public opinion, and to his own calculations, under these, of his own interest, are under the arbitrary control of any other human being, by whatever name called. This is the essence of slavery, and what distinguishes it from freedom. A domestic, a civil, a political slave, in the plain unsophisticated sense of the word—in no metaphorical sense—is every married woman. No matter with what wealth she may be surrounded, with what dainties she may be fed, with what splendor of trappings adorned, with what voluptuousness her corporeal, mental, or moral sweets may be gathered; that high prerogative of human nature, the faculty of self-government, the basis of intellectual developement, without which no moral conduct can exist, is to her wanting. The high-minded would pine and die under such degradation; or boldly, at whatever risk, break the infernal bond of slavery. Therefore has the cold-blooded system annihilated even the very possibility of the acquisition of *mind* in its victims. They submit, suffer, laugh, and enjoy when and as much as they are permitted, torment by petty vices and failings their masters and each other, and are dead to the very suspicion of the elysium of happiness, of which the system of inequality, slavery, and degradation, deprives them and their masters. Were one of these masters, were a man, for the sake of all the luxurious pampering with which art could supply him, to yield to a woman the control over those of his actions which the law permitted to be voluntary, to go in and out, to dress and address at her bidding, *obedient* in every thing to her smile or frown—who amongst men, or peradventure amongst women, is there, that would not exclaim against the baseness of such a sacrifice on the part of man?

What! to be debarred from the air, or the society of his fellow-creatures, to be liable to that *imprisonment*, which the law awards as a punishment for crime—often the most atrocious in severity—for no offence, at the mere capricious bidding of a fellow-creature, of a woman: not to think for himself, to act for himself? to presume to exercise no reciprocal control over the actions of that woman, however pernicious to his well-being, to whose control all of his were subjected? obedience, uninquiring, unresisting, his only law? his very propensities to be obedient, not to move for his own gratification, but for the exclusive gratification of another? What *man* could long endure to live on such terms? Who could bear up under the load of scorn which such submission, which such a sacrifice of the high intellectual and moral faculty of self-government would bring upon him, for the dastard gratification, meted out at another's will, of his mere animal propensities, himself waited upon, clad, and fed, to swell the train and pamper the enjoyments of another as often as caprice might urge his keeper to the use of his charms and graces, of mind or of body? If it be pretended that the sting of the disgrace and misery consists not in the actual submission, but in the submission to a *woman*, who of men is there that would submit on such terms the control over his actions to any man? who, without being base, without losing the individuality and the virtue of his character, could make such a sacrifice to any man, to any human being? What makes the evil more, when submitted to, in this country, from a woman than from a man? The difference is a mere evil of the imagination: it is altogether the result of what is called public opinion, of the public opinion of the oppressors, of the males of the human race in their own favor. In countries where ordinary labor is performed by black slaves, is the misery of the slaves incalculably, or at all increased, when the ownership happens to be in a woman? In Turkey and the Barbary piratical States, are the evils of slavery found to be degradingly increased by the white male slaves when their owner happens to be a woman? Is it not apt to be alleviated when the owner, whether man or woman, happens to form an attachment to the slave? In these cases public opinion is impartial, and estimates the *real evils* of slavery, whether suffered by man or woman, whether inflicted by man or woman, in the scale of justice. Capabilities of enjoying and suffering the same, privations or means of privation the same, why should the real evil of slavery be less to woman than to man? The constrained habit of endurance on the part of women, the perverse notion of fitness thence arising, and the public opinion of the oppressors, are the real and only differences in the case. The real evils of constraint are as great in the one case as in the other. The pleasures of freedom which the slave might enjoy are no less real, no less felt by those who are free, no less a drawback from the happiness which the slave might enjoy, because he is so debased as not even to be able to perceive them. As the pleasures of sight would add to the happiness of the blind, so would the pleasures of freedom add to the happiness of the slave, though previously unsuspecting the existence of such enjoyments. Reject then this partial and factitious public opinion of oppression, and the real evils of constraint will appear as they are, really less when suffered by man under the control of woman, than when suffered by woman under the control of man. When woman is the sufferer, and the power of control is in the hands of man, she, being the weaker in physical strength, has no point of support, is forced in every thing to submit; but when the power of control is in the hands of the woman, the want of superior physical strength to enforce on all occasions her commands, and the possession of this physical power of resistance by man, over whom the commands are exercised, must beget such consideration, such mildness of control, as is in vain sought where all fear of the possibility of resistance to commands ever so arbitrary is removed. An adult human being, though a woman, and though a wife, is possessed of all the senses, the appetites, the faculties and capabilities of enjoyment, of any other adult human being. To hold the gratification of these and of all power over her voluntary actions at the bidding of another, deprives her of more than half the happiness which she might enjoy, though such debasing and unnecessary power were ever so kindly exercised. She either feels it, and is more or less miserable, if not relieved by the pleasures of intellectual superiority; or is reduced to a state of stupidity and apathy, rendering her incapable of a greater degree of happiness than that of the brutes.

Such is the glorious triumph which man obtains by rendering woman, in marriage, the voluntary slave of his sensual appetites and all his caprices! He surrenders the delights of equality, namely those of esteem, of friendship, of intellectual and sympathetic intercourse, for the vulgar pleasure of command. By the continued practice of domestic caprice and despotism, by the habit of substituting force for reason, of making his own will the standard of rectitude, of neglecting the cultivation of the art of reasoning, of persuasion, and of the pleasures of sympathy, by

Qu. 1.] *Marriage Vow of Slavery, a superfluous Insult.* 71

constantly referring all actions to himself alone as possessing that interest which ought to be, in his law-supported estimation, their exclusive object, the whole moral structure of the mind of *man* is perverted. His pride and selfishness are habitually raised to their highest standard. The monarch of the domestic circle, he would be the monarch of every circle he meets. He has been rendered incapable of considering the effects of his actions on all whose interests they may reach: he calculates their effects with reference to himself alone. In his intercourse with the world at large, he carries forth that rule of force and notion of the superior importance of his own happiness to that of all around, which leads him in all his actions to substitute power for right; and which, continually checked and opposed by similar pretensions of his fellow-men, equally formed by domestic despotism, is one of the most fruitful and perennial causes of personal annoyance, mutual depredation, and misery. Such fruits let man continue to reap from his baneful lust of uncontrolled power!

How totally unnecessary this forced vow, at the altar, of voluntary obedience, how totally useless to secure the uncontrolled domination of man, as husband, under the social arrangements which he has formed, the case of daughters will amply testify. Adult daughters not only do not, when they come of age, undertake a vow of obedience to their fathers, but the law expressly exonerates them from any sort of obedience. No direct restraints on locomotion or on any other voluntary action, no power of imprisonment, no control as to friends or acquaintances, no domestic powers to be backed if necessary by the whole physical force of the law, do fathers possess over their daughters. The adult daughters of a family may moreover, in their mother and in each other, find a support against the despotism of the father. And yet, notwithstanding these advantages of law and situation, the control of the father over the actions of the daughter is generally as complete as over those of the wife, and for the same reason; because the father has the command of all those circumstances, of all those means, which would be necessary to enable a daughter to avail herself of those immunities from arbitrary control which the law gives her. If she dare to disobey, if she presume to regulate any of her own actions, as the law permits her, according to her own notions of prudence and propriety, the father can dismiss her from his household and leave her to starve, or to run such risks of starving and other misery, from the helpless way in which her sex is brought up, as will be only secondary in terror to the imagination to absolute starvation. Such irresistible influence does the command of property, of the means of living, supported by the early habits of education, possess! Daughters then make no vow, but are supported, like sons, by law, in disobedience, as often as they think the wishes of their fathers immoral or incompatible with their happiness. Yet are adult daughters, though not the legal, the actual slaves of their fathers; slaves through circumstances more powerful than law, slaves through arrangements formed by other branches of this same law, which render nugatory the vain permission of disobedience. If then, from the mere command of wealth, education, helplessness in providing for themselves, and public opinion, adult daughters are in point of fact controlled at the caprice of their fathers, without any vow, even without any law to enforce obedience, nay in spite of the law sanctioning and upholding disobedience, how utterly hopeless must be the lot of wives, parcelled out one to each man, a stronger being than herself, where wealth, education, public opinion in favor of man's despotism, are strengthened by a marriage-slave-code bringing back woman at marriage to the state of a childish automaton, though no *vow* of obedience were exacted, though no vile pretext of voluntariness on the part of the slave were set up by the oppressor! Was the reason of this constrained vow a residue of shame on the part of the framers of this unequal, cruel, and cowardly code over physical weakness, lest they should be reproached with the enormity of the misuse of force, sheltering their iniquity under the pretended consent of each of their victims? To erect uninquiring obedience into a duty, to weave it into a pretended code of morals, to degrade the mind into an acquiescence in injustice, is the last triumph of unrelenting despotism, rarely exacted from ordinary slaves, and reserved, without any sort of necessity, for the degradation of the domestic female slave in marriage.

Will it be said that more power of control is requisite over wives than over daughters, because that habits of early obedience in childhood having been acquired by daughters towards their fathers, but not by wives towards their husbands, such additional power is requisite to counterbalance the want of previously acquired habits of obedience? First prove that obedience without persuasion is requisite for the happiness of any rational adult human being, of the one commanding more than of the one commanded: then prove that such obedience is requisite to the happiness of the husband; and when you have done this, nothing is yet effected to justify the husband's despotism or power of restraint. Prove that the happiness of *the wife* is promoted by vesting in any other human being all power of control over her own voluntary actions. Till this is done, all other proofs are impertinences: for if it be justifiable, to increase the happiness of the husband, that he should be gratified with the power of controlling by force his wife's actions; why should it not be equally justifiable, in order to increase the happiness of the wife, to gratify her with the power of controlling, if necessary by force of the law, her husband's actions? Is it that women brought up under the present debasing system, would not derive as much vicious pleasure (pleasure productive, all its consequences considered, of preponderant evil) from the exercise of such authority over their fellow-creatures, as men, brought up under the same system, now derive? On the contrary, as in proportion to weakness and ignorance are known to be the pleasures of mere arbitrary command, so with the most weak and the most ignorant they would be the highest. It is no more fitting, it tends no more to increase the aggregate of human happiness, that the happiness of wives should be dependent on the good-will of husbands, wise or foolish, than that the happiness of husbands, including their power of regulating their own actions, should depend on the caprices of wives, however foolish or wise. Each individual has an equal claim to the exercise of all the means of happiness in its power, not encroaching on similar claims in others. The assumption however of want of habits of obedience in the wife, is altogether unfounded: for the general habit of obedience as women and daughters having been implanted, and the mind having been always trained to look forward to the transference of these habits to the husband, who is supposed to bring a healing balm of joy to repay the sacrifice, the stranger husband derives as much advantage from the habit as if he had been all his life the particular object in whose favor it had been contracted.

If then it has been shown that the interest of the adult daughter is no more, nor in any other way, involved in the happiness of the father than that of any other branch of his household, and not by any means as much so involved as that of the sons, how much more evident is it that the happiness of the wife is not involved in that of the husband, all protection of law (except as to extreme abuse of despotic power, as in other slave cases,) being withdrawn from her, and an oath of servitude, under the sanction of superstition, enjoined and exacted!

We might here perhaps rest satisfied with the refutation of this monstrous fiction of male despotism, that the interest of wives is necessarily involved in that of their husbands. If it be meant that their happiness or misery are dependent on those in whose power both positive law and the indirect operation of institutions have placed them, nothing can be more true; but nothing can be more insignificant to the point in question. They are dependent indeed: happiness or misery rises or falls with the variations in the will of him who possesses uncontrolled power, and who, as the "Article" declares, by a grand governing law of human nature is inclined to extend that power till those subjected to it are reduced at least to the state of the negroes in the West Indies. How then can that will, without control, be as necessarily directed to consult the happiness of the person subjected to it as of the agent himself? Such must be the meaning of the mysterious term "involved", or it can have no meaning available to the argument. This can only be proved by a reference to facts. If the disposition to promote the happiness of another to an equal degree with our own exist, and the same power be applicable to both, the happiness of both will be in point of fact equally promoted. Happiness is the aggregate; of which pleasures are the items. Do wives enjoy as many pleasures of all sorts as their husbands, having the guardianship of their volitions, do? This is the experimental touchstone to prove or disprove an identity of interest, or an involving, as it is called, of the happiness of one human being in that of another. Let us go through the different pleasures of which rational sentient beings are susceptible. First, of the senses and internal excitement: the husband possessed of almost unlimited power, that of personal restraint over his wife (limited only by direct injury to life or limb), and that of commanding all the means of gratifying the desires springing from these sources, does he, in point of fact, afford the woman under his control an equal extent of these enjoyments with himself? It is so notorious that he does not do so, that he has made, every where, what he calls his system of morals to coincide with his practice. The same indulgence in sensual pleasures which is freely permitted to himself and his associates, is held quite unseemly in his weaker companion. Eating or drinking to excess, either in quantity or quality of food, which is regarded by many as the prerogative of man rich enough to enjoy them, or to be limited only by a prudential regard to immediate health, is looked upon as disgusting in woman: whereas, if wives had an equality of enjoyment in this respect with their masters, excess would be in public opinion *equally pernicious* and vicious in both. Wives would be advanced to an equality of useful enjoyment, of enjoyment, all its

Qu.1.] *Pleasures of Senses deemed immoral in Women.* 77

consequences to all parties liable to be affected by it considered, with their husbands; and both wives and husbands would be equally restrained from all indulgences productive of preponderant evil, effects on health and all other consequences taken into the account: the conduct of each would, as to these indulgences, be equally regulated by individual notions of prudence and propriety. Now the conduct of the husband alone is regulated by such calculations of his own; while that of the wife is restrained by his arbitrary will, just as he restrains his children. Not only at home, to which the wife is mostly confined, does this inequality of indulgence prevail, but to a still greater degree abroad; man—in marriage—having the exclusive command of the purse and the power of imprisoning without trial or any alleged offence, his wife. While the wife is imprisoned at home (the wife of the richest as well as of the poorest man in the country, if he so think fit to direct), counting or swallowing her sorrows, or playing with bird, kitten, needle, or novel, the husband is enjoying abroad the manly pleasures of conviviality, to wit, epicurism, drunkenness, and obscene or foolish jargon of conversation; from which women are by these self-denying moralists wisely excluded, lest their habitual and unnaturally-forced reserve should check the overflowings of such manly animal gratifications. Their more appropriate business, as defined by the vile system of sexual morality, is to remain patiently at home waiting for the happy moment to welcome the sated despot, happy if the want of external excitement subsides into mere ennui, and does not vent itself on the slave in some of the endless modes of displaying the caprice of uncontrolled power. As to sexual pleasures, so iniquitous is the inequality, so enormous the hypocrisy of the pretended marriage contract, that one party, endowed by nature with equal capabilities and desires of enjoyment, and by education and circumstances with more liability to the pains and pleasures of sexual sympathy, is debarred by the public opinion of man formed in his own favor, from even murmuring at the neglects and irregularities of the other; while any neglect or irregularity on her part towards her master having the power is first punished, at his arbitrary domestic caprice, by using any of the numberless physical restraints and modes of mental torture within his reach, then by the cruelty of positive law, and last of all by public opinion hunting the victim by malice and ill offices to despair and pining, or to sudden death. The infidelity of the husband (essentially involving the happiness of the wife) to any extent, must be patiently borne by the wife; she has no redress, physical, legal, or of public opinion. The infidelity of the wife (scarcely abstracting from the mass of pleasures of the husband) in a single instance, is revenged by the husband with a complication of punishments, greater than those accorded by law to many of the most atrocious crimes. This is not the occasion to show the wickedness because the immense preponderance of misery, ensuing from such inequality of enjoyment and punishment, domestic, legal and moral; but simply to show the fact that the happiness of wives is not involved in that of their husbands, is not promoted to the same extent as their own. Another opportunity will perhaps be taken for treating this question more at large. The discussion must now be limited to the extraordinary assertions and inferences of the "Article."

The simple pleasures of the other senses, smelling,

feeling or touch, hearing, and seeing, unimportant as they are, compared with those of taste and sex, follow the same rule of distribution in marriage. One of the parties, the husband, has the exclusive command over them, enjoying as much as he pleases of them himself, and permitting the use of whatever portion of them he thinks fit to his companion. These pleasures, however, are mostly enjoyed in association with other pleasures, chiefly those of intellect and sympathy. As to intellect, man, to fit his slave for the vow and the practice of blind obedience, deprives her of all means of knowledge except such crumbs as, like the sparrow, she may pick up from her master's table. As to sympathy, the *power of imprisonment* which man in marriage holds, cuts off his household slave from all sympathy but with himself, his children, and cats or other household animals. To some lighter public or private amusements where these associated pleasures may be enjoyed, husbands occasionally *permit* their wives, as they do children, to have access; but from all scenes, assemblies, and incidents, that could really enlarge their minds or sympathies, they are, partly by positive law, partly by man's public opinion, backed by persecution, effectually excluded. Home, except on a few occasions, chiefly for the drillings of superstition to render her obedience more submissive, is the eternal prison-house of the wife: the husband paints it as the abode of calm bliss, but takes care to find, out-side of doors, for his own use, a species of bliss not quite so calm, but of a more varied and stimulating description. These are facts of such daily occurrence and notoriety, that to the multitudinous, unreflecting, creatures, their victims, they pass by as the established order of nature.

From intellectual, from social or sympathetic pleasures, which so elevate the human race in the scale of being and capability of happiness over all other animals, which so increase, by intwining themselves with, all the simple pleasures of the senses, which occupy so great a space of time and human life with gentle and never over-exciting emotion, which are so cheap of purchase, requiring nothing but culture for their enjoyment, women, and particularly wives, are brutally excluded, with the real but vain object of adding to man's voluptuous enjoyments, and of pampering his conceit of superiority and his unhallowed love of despotic command. From want of education, of early culture, *equal to that of men,* in every branch of useful knowledge, women lose the immense accession to their happiness which intellectual culture would afford them. From hours and nights and days of interesting conversation, they are excluded : to silence or retirement they are driven, while the males are glowing with interest, enjoying the emotions of curiosity, judgement, anticipation. Besides the total loss to women, how much would man's enjoyment of these pleasures be increased, by doubling the number of persons capable of sharing them with him, and of associating them with so many other pleasures! From the seclusion from events and knowledge in which women are brought up, and from the ignorance which is thus forced upon them, the herd of men unavoidably contract an habitual contempt for their intellectual powers, and repress as presumption an opinion, even timidly given by them, on any subject beyond the grasp of children's minds. Does it tend to the happiness of women, of wives, to be the objects of this never-ceasing contempt? Is not the happiness of every human being necessarily increased by the respect of those by whom it is surrounded? and is there any respect so exquisitely felt and so useful as that which the culture and diffusion of intellectual power insure to the intelligent? But the pleasures of intellectual communication, of interchange of thought and speculation, are but a part of those lost by women from that intellectual imbecility into which man's perverse notions of selfish interest drill them. Those private and vacant hours, during which the mind of the husband is excited abroad wherever his inclinations prompt him—whether in pursuit of gain, science, or amusement—are passed drearily by the wife for want of intellectual resources. The vacuum of an unemployed mind is not simply the absence of happiness; it is a state of positive torment, if not directed to malignant or otherwise mischievous low pursuits, which in general re-act on the happiness of the husband and of all those within the sphere of their influence. Intellectual pursuits would not only supply an occupation for these hours, but would lay in a fund of materials for thought, which would become associated with simpler occupations, and convert all simple into *compounded* pleasures, or supply pleasing trains of thought for those occasions of seclusion and self-dependence into which accident throws, more or less, every individual. All the other benefits arising from intellectual culture, particularly from the acquisition of physical knowledge, as freedom from superstitious terrors, from imposture and dupery, from physical evils to health and comfort, might here be enumerated to swell the loss to the happiness of women from this source; namely, from that intellectual imbecility to which they are systematically if not perfidiously trained. Some women there are, who, from a peculiar and fortunate animal temperament, or from mere insensibility of nerve, or from the lowest ignorance, cannot comprehend, much less estimate, the loss of happiness they suffer from this source. But apathy is not happiness : better certainly not to feel than to be wretched. The object of a just philosophy, however, is not to exterminate sensation, is not to reduce sentient beings to the state of unorganized matter, but to raise those whose organization renders them sentient, and capable of becoming rational, creatures, to the highest state of habitual enjoyment of which their nature is susceptible. Our immediate question is, whether men, *i. e.* husbands, permit as great a quantity of these intellectual enjoyments to their wives as they themselves indulge in. From no class of human pleasures are women in general and wives in particular more systematically excluded. When a few of them, in spite of exclusions, pick up a few crumbs of real knowledge, they are looked upon as intruders and usurpers of the rights and privileges necessarily appertaining to strength, of the more brawny, and therefore of the superior, sex.

If from intellectual pleasures we turn to those of sympathy, or of the social class, we shall find a contrast almost as marked and barefaced between the enjoyments of the two parties, husbands and wives. Here shall we find exemplified to the letter the operation of the " grand pri- " mary law of human nature—that men exercising power " without checks will reduce those subjected to it to the " state, at least, of the slaves in the West Indies." Truly at least as grievous. Uninformed men, the creatures of the unfavorable circumstances which have developed their characters, have in many important respects, and those the most closely connected with individual happiness, reduced women in the state of wives, to a social condition even more slavish than that of the female West India slaves. Amongst slaves, one common stock, that of the master, supporting, however miserably yet equably, the whole population, women, children, and men, the female slaves have not been under the necessity of submitting to a second state of individual domestic slavery to the male slaves, for the privilege of sharing unequally with them the means of a wretched existence derived from their united labors. No female slave is obliged, for the sake of existence, to vow obedience to all the despotic commands of a male slave, to resign her privileges, such as the task-master leaves to all, of going out and coming in, of moving from place to place within the desolate sphere of common bonds, of forming acquaintance, friendship, and attachment, at her pleasure, with any individuals of her fellow-slaves, just as the males form their acquaintances, friendships, and attachments amongst their fellow-slaves, and particularly, that most inestimable privilege of all, the basis of all improvement, morality, and happiness—of moulding her own actions according to her own views of interest, propriety and justice, liable to the same physical, legal, and arbitrary restraints with her male companion in slavery, and no more. To none of these evils of individual domestic despotism, peculiar and superadded to the common evils of slavery, is the female slave in the West Indies subjected. From none of these peculiar and superadded evils of domestic slavery is the wife, however gorgeously attired, in those termed civilized communities, exempt. The wife, at marriage, is constrained to the immoral vow of obedience to the arbitrary will of the husband: the physical strength of the husband, the iron dictates of law and superstition, and the more unrelenting malice of male-created public opinion, enforce the debasing performance of this extorted vow. Is there a wife who dares to form her own acquaintances amongst women or men, without the permission, direct or indirect, of the husband to form such acquaintances, or to retain them when formed? Is there a husband who would not spurn the permission, direct or implied, of the wife to form or retain such acquaintances? Is there a female slave in the West Indies who would submit to such dictation from any male slave, if her companion, her equal, and no more than her equal, in degradation and misery? Is there a wife of civilized society who can dream to advance beyond acquaintances, to the formation of friendships with other women or with men, without the express approbation of her husband? Is there a husband who would not laugh at the impertinence of his wife who should venture an opinion on matters so much beyond her capacity of judgement, as to the persons with whom, men or women, he might think proper to form the strictest bonds of friendship? From friendship, if we proceed to attachments, persecution desolation and death attend the footsteps of the wife if the husband only *suspect* them, (for permission or even connivance is not only here out of the question, but to look for it would be deemed insanity on the part of the wife, and to grant it would be deemed on the part of the husband degradation and immorality,) though his own attachments were as extensive and public as those of any Eastern despot. Is there, on the contrary, any husband who would not conceive his right of sovereignty, his power to make wretched, the badge of his manhood, compromised, by permitting his wife to pry into or interfere with his attach-

Qu. 1.] *Power of Imprisonment debars Wives.* 85

ments or connexions amongst men or women? Cut off and isolated from all human society and social endearment is the wife, except in as far as the husband permits. Without legal, moral, or physical power to restrain, the wife is compelled silently to witness and to smother her repinings, whatever extravagancies of unbridled libertinism the husband may think proper to indulge in ; happy if she escape the further consequential evils of violence and disease, the natural attendants on his misgoverned passions. From the common abode the wife dares not stray without the husband's permission : it is a peculiar courtesy and condescension in the husband to deign to inform the wife when or where he goes, how long or where he will stay or when he will return. The house is *his* house with every thing in it; and of all fixtures the most abjectly his is his breeding machine, the wife. In *his* house he imprisons her or opens the doors at his option ; an indulgent master is all she can look for : the right to go in or out belongs to her as much as to the kitten or the child with whose sports she is associated, and to the level of whose sympathies she is condemned. No female slave in the West Indies is compelled to submit to such petty domestic despotism as this : to the common lot of civil slavery she submits equally with her male companion; but by that male companion and equal in slavery no inquisitorial despotism is usurped over her, in order to compensate to the stronger and dastard male for his submission to the chains of his master. Herself and her children are equally provided for with him, equally though scantily, by their common master. With the trifles of domestic conduct unconnected with labor, the common master has no motive to interfere. The same liberty in these matters, because unimportant to the interest of the master, that the male slave enjoys, the female slave enjoys also. She is not bound like the wife of what is called civilization, for the sake of a scanty and precarious support from the hand of her male companion, to make to him a second vow of domestic thraldom: the same liberty of acquaintance, of friendship, of attachment, the same right to go out and come in, to regulate all her own actions by her own notions of interest and propriety that her male companion is permitted to enjoy, she enjoys also. Her destiny is not aggravated beyond that of the male by the never-closing eye of a domestic tyrant, jealous and brutal, because having power with impunity to be so, hemming round not only her actions but her words and thoughts at his pleasure, and invested by law with all the uncontrolled power requisite to keep life in such a constant state of torment, that the morning sun that calls her to a renewal of existence may be cursed for its summons to a renewal of misery.

And yet this state of the civilized wife, worse than that of the female West India slave, is termed a state of equality, of identity of interest, of involving of interests with those of her husband, her master! so termed by logicians, by philosophers! When by such phrases, logicians and philosophers, and those the advocates of the principle of Utility, blind themselves as to facts of every day's occurrence, can we wonder at the impenetrable hardness of heart of the bulk of men as to the destiny and happiness of half their race? their education, superstition, and public opinion, all coinciding with their most imperious passions, love of pleasure and love of power, in rendering women their abject slaves, and imputing to nature the imbecility, the folly, and the vices, which their own hands have nurtured and matured in the creatures which their institutions have formed? Such miseries does despotism, public or domestic, necessarily weave for itself: where it expected to enjoy a quiet submission, it reaps suspicion, cunning, lying, hypocrisy, and hate. Social happiness cannot breathe but in the air of equality.

Will it be said that civilized wives are superior in point of social liberty to female West India slaves, inasmuch as they enjoy the common protection with their male keepers of the general laws of the country? No statement was ever more egregiously false. Whether as to person or to property, wives are cut off (a few flagrant and rarely occurring cases excepted) from the common protection of the laws. Property, *as wife*, she has none, nor of course any more rights with respect to property than the children of the household. The husband alone must sue and be sued. The arbitrary power in the hands of the husband cutting her off from all intercourse with her fellow-creatures, isolating her, like the domestic cat afraid of pursuit in the street, to the eternal prison of the husband's house, she can never please or displease, molest or be molested by, the individuals of ordinary society, *except as permitted by her keeper*. From social pleasures with all other human beings, particularly males, the husband has the power of effectually excluding her, and does in fact as to all independence and happiness exclude her. From these, from whom she is debarred, the law affects to give her equal protection! From the husband, to whose restraints and wrongs all her actions, words and thoughts are exposed, the law affords her no protection at all; starvation and blows endangering life (so rarely capable of proof, and the complaint so easily by the domestic indissoluble despot avenged) excepted. Protection indeed! It is made a part of what is called her moral duty to submit to the orders, just or unjust, of her master: she is made to *swear obedience* to domestic slavery. Talk to such an isolated and dependent being of protection of the laws against evils which do not to her exist, which are altogether swallowed up in the unmitigated, uncompensated, evil of abject, hopeless, submission, prostration of affections, understanding, and will, to the unchecked and non-accountable caprices of the silliest and vilest of mankind if by chance her husband!—what is it but the most heartless of insults, the most flagrant and threadbare hypocrisy? To civilized married women, the protection of laws against society at large is absolutely nugatory : be the laws ever so benevolent, ever so wise, while woman remains a domestic slave, she cannot be benefited by them. The female West India slave is liable to the *occasional* despotic will, to the lust or caprice of the common tyrant of all : the civilized wife is liable to the uncontrolled and eternal caprices of an ever-jealous and ever-present tyrant : a tyrant, beneficent *if he pleases*, but still a tyrant because he retains the uncontrolled *power* of being wicked, of making his fellow-creature wretched, at his pleasure. Till laws afford married women the same protection against the restraints and violence of the men to whom they are married, that they affect to afford them against all other individuals; till they afford them the same protection against the restraints and violence of their husbands, that their husbands enjoy against their caprices and violence, the social condition of the civilized wife will remain more completely slavish than that of the female slave of the

West Indies; and triumphantly will remain established, here amongst us, without travelling to the East or the West in pursuit of it, the truth of Mr. Mill's position, that "men possessing power without checks will necessa-"rily use it at the expense of others till they reduce them "to the state, at least, of the slaves in the West Indies."

Now supposing that husbands, having the power, were in the habit of *permitting* to their wives equal enjoyment in the pleasures of taste and sex, equal enjoyment of all the other senses, simple and associated with the pleasures of intelligence, sympathy and benevolence, equal license of locomotion, equal right of intercourse with other human beings, with themselves; what would be the consequence? that wives would be as happy as husbands? By no means: very far from it. The wife would still enjoy but the pleasures of the slave, however varied. Caprice may withhold them at a moment's notice: but this is not all. Of all our pleasures none is so delightful, so requisite to the enjoyment of all our other pleasures, as that of voluntariness, of regulating our actions according to our own views of interest and duty, and by our own will. This superior and universally associated pleasure is lost to the slave, ever so pampered with *permitted* enjoyments. With the power of self-government, of acting *without permission*, are also lost the occasions of unfolding and exercising the mental powers, and of exercising any moral act. No mechanical or commanded mode of action can be moral, except as to the mind that foresees, orders, or puts in motion the machine that performs it. Voluntariness is requisite for morality. That self-approbation which accompanies and follows the performance of a virtuous act, arising from the consciousness of the successful exertion of our own mental powers in producing a result of preponderant good; that peculiar zest of sympathy which arises from the contemplation of the happiness which we have *voluntarily*, and not as machines, co operated to produce—are lost to the wife, as to any other human being, whose actions and beneficence are regulated by the judgement and volition of any other human being whatever. And yet these are the pleasures which, above all others, are requisite to real, to exalted happiness. The hammer and the shears may be made to co-operate in any design of intelligence and benevolence, as well as the wife divested like them of the power of self-regulation. But are they therefore happy? The only happiness beyond these inanimate co-operators the obsequious wife can enjoy, is the pleasure of being favorably regarded by the despot at whose bidding her actions are regulated. Over every act, over every pleasure of life, does this charm of self-regulation and voluntarinesss diffuse a heightened gratification. All pleasures, without them, are those of the unconscious ox, who consumes the food provided by his keeper and sleeps, but thinks not. With them, all pleasures have an intellectual glow: they resemble the enjoyments which industrious skill has procured for itself, of which the mere animal part is perhaps the least poignant of the ingredients. All the intervals of action they fill up with a consciousness of self-respect, of the pleasing exercise of intellectual power.

As long therefore as barbarous laws permit one human being under the name of husband to retain another human being, adult like himself, under the name of wife, in a state of slavery; or in other words, as long as they subject her actions and pleasures, powers of locomotion and social intercourse, to the arbitrary regulation of the husband; so long will it be impossible for a husband under a system of such iniquitous despotism to impart, by his permission, equal happiness to his wife with that which he enjoys, or has the power of enjoying. He is restrained by the laws alone, which, if ever so vile, cannot be always present to torment him. She is equally restrained, in some cases more severely, by the laws than he is. By superstition and public opinion all her actions and enjoyments are a thousandfold more restrained than his. But over and above all these equal or more galling restraints, all the remaining actions of the wife are subjected to the husband's despotic control! Till he divests himself of this unlimited *power* of making miserable, that is to say, of being wicked at his pleasure, without any accountability, without any protection to his victim, he cannot, if he would, make her as happy as himself. He must extract the poison that lurks in every concession: he must exchange the pleasures of the despot for those of the friend and the equal. From a person who is not permitted to judge, determine and act for herself, are taken away the *occasions*, the incidents, for the calling forth and exercising the intellectual powers. Without these incidents and this power of determining, the judgement on moral subjects, on subjects of action, can no more be developed, than the arts of dancing or music can be taught without practice. No morality or immorality can attach to the acts of a constrained agent, but to him who constrains those actions. Until man therefore resigns his withering despotism, he cannot enjoy the intercourse of intelligence and beneficence: if the possession of these qualities in his companion tend more to his happiness than stupidity and petty vexatious vices in that companion, he must pay the price of his enjoyment, and make his slave his equal.

Another feature in the condition of wives, under the slave or marriage code of civilized society, as contrasted with that of husbands, and exemplifying in a very striking way the poetical beauties of the involving of interests, will be found in the tremendous vicissitudes of wealth and consideration to which almost all women are exposed as the ordinary lot of their lives. The husband, possessing every thing, wealth, skill, intelligence; when he dies, the surviving wife is reduced almost always to comparative poverty, frequently to absolute and biting want. By the death of the wife, on the contrary, the husband has one less to support; and with undiminished pecuniary and other means of enjoyment and exertion he begins as it were life again, and smiles on the next willing victim trained like the self-immolating widows of Hindostan by superstition, public opinion, and want, offering her fortune, if she have any, and her personal liberty, to his caprice, for the participation of whatever species of lodging, clothing, food, and sexual indulgence, he may condescend to favor her with. To whatever vicissitudes the casualties or vices of the husband may condemn him, the wife is equally condemned: and for the most part in her is then found the firmness of endurance, in her are found the consolation and support of the husband in distress. Besides all such common calamities, the wife has more than an equal chance, being generally younger, of bearing the peculiar vicissitude and calamity arising from comparative poverty, or absolute want, and diminished respect, if not absolute neglect and contempt, at the husband's death. Frequently to be sure, her *happiness* is not diminished by this casualty, as she may gain more (her wretched existence being always but an alternative of evils) by freedom from a hated yoke, than lose by diminution of physical comforts, or of such cold and distant respect as mere station is apt to command. From the habit of unrepining suffering, from the utter fruitlessness of complaint, women, and particularly wives, smile under calamities, which the ever-enjoying and always unrestrained and therefore impatient males are unable with decent composure to bear. Evils are not less evils though heroically borne. Let our admiration of and sympathy with the heroic victims of domestic despotism and unequal laws, afford us an additional motive to aid in the utter extinction of these most prolific sources of human misery. What *man* can bear the vicissitude of sudden loss of fortune with serenity of mind? how frequently does it plunge him into either sudden self-destruction or gradual waste of the mental and animal powers!

The very difference in the organization and in the acquired dispositions of women from those of men—for all their present peculiarities and defects, like those of men, are the mere result of the vicious circumstances surrounding and acting upon them—at the same time indispose, and render it more difficult for, a man to use power in promoting the happiness of a woman than of a fellow-creature organized exactly like himself. As to mere sexual sympathies on both sides from desire of mutual enjoyment, they soon become reduced, under the existing system of restraint and despotism in marriage, to their mere animal proportions and importance, occupying and influencing perhaps a twenty-fourth of time, thought, and action, and causing perhaps, in some of the most happily developed minds of the males, a temporary suspension of the indulgence of individual feelings and mere personal gratification, the necessary result of despotic power. The great bulk of men, however, from the wretched training in which they have been brought up, necessarily pursue mere individual selfish gratification on the very bosom of love, their sexual feelings having nothing of *sympathy* in them. Nay, some are brutal enough to associate—and as a point of morals too!—antipathy towards their companions who presume to share unreservedly and affectionately in their enjoyments; passive endurance being in their minds the perfection of conduct in their slaves! How, therefore, with the minor incidents and feelings of women arising from peculiarity of organization, unconnected with male desire, can man be expected to sympathize? seldom is it that he can even know them. He can only know them by guess or from description: he cannot appreciate them from past or present similarity of feeling, as he can do when the feelings of a fellow-man are concerned; with whom he can entirely sympathize. Hence an insurmountable obstacle in the way of either sex exercising power to promote the happiness of those of the other sex as effectually as they could their own, even supposing the same inclination to exist. Though the interest, as of two partners in business, as to pecuniary matters and other gross concerns, might be the same, though the organization and sympathies were the same—who would ever think of asserting that uncontrolled power, or any power, lodged in the hands of the one partner to regulate the actions of the other, could by possibility be equally productive of happiness to that other with the same power lodged in his own hands, though both lived in the same house and ate at the same table? The one could not promote the happiness of the other in all those minute circumstances on which happiness depends, without knowing always the state of feelings and wishes of that other. In order to know these, he must constantly consult that other as to the state of his wishes, and be guided by them in case of his not convincing the other of their inexpediency to his happiness. But if this were always done, what would be the use of the power of control? A power never exercised, and never to be exercised, is only a dead letter: the power would be in fact surrendered. If then the power of man over man, where an identity of organization, of pecuniary and other obvious interests, exists, cannot be exercised so as to promote the happiness of that other without in fact surrendering such power; how much more absurd is it to suppose that where, from difference of organization and of sympathy, as in the case of a wife, additional difficulties are thrown in the way of ascertaining or sympathizing with another person's minute wishes, such power can be exercised so as to promote the happiness of the person subjected to it! How much more are these difficulties increased when we take into account the peculiarities of disposition and character of women, opposed in so many respects, from a difference of culture and from withholding the means of knowledge, to those of men! The impossibility increases to infinity. In truth, those delicate shades of feeling and wishes on which happiness, particularly in domestic life, depends, are altogether withered by the rude gaze of inquiry. The necessity of consulting and obtaining the approbation of a master to their enjoyment, represses them altogether; and either apathy and insensibility succeed in the mind of the slave, or concealment and all the expedients of cunning prevail; or a curious mixture of apathy and cunning is resorted to, to avoid or retaliate for the humiliation of suing for petty favors; where no power of granting or refusing any favors should exist, where nothing but perfect equality of reason and affection should regulate and restrain the feelings and wishes of both parties, neither having power to constrain the wishes of the other, neither in return wishing to act in a way to lessen the happiness of the other. Such would be the result of freedom and of a perfect equality of rights and duties between two persons of the same or different sexes living together! such can never be the effect of constraint, where the one is dependent on the other!

So certain is the fact that dissimilarity of organization between any two sentient beings tends to decrease, instead of, as by the argument of the "Article" vainly supposed, to render stronger the sympathy between them; that this very dissimilarity of organization between the sexes has been made use of as one of the most ordinary pretexts, to justify the stronger party in withholding from the weaker an equality of enjoyments and imposing on them more onerous obligations. It is a fact extending through all animal nature, and most easy of explanation, that the sympathy or antipathy of all races increases or diminishes in proportion to similarity or dissimilarity of organization. Not only is this the case as between the different genera, but even between the different species of animals, and particularly so between the different species of the human race, though colour, scarcely noticed amongst other animals, should be the only point of distinction. On difference of colour is chiefly founded the antipathy between the blacks and whites and other shades in the human race. Any variation from the usual organization is termed *monstrous*, and regarded with antipathy, though no evil arise from it. Were no source of pleasure connected with the difference of organization of men and women, it is very probable that the antipathies between them would have been such that they would either have formed different communities, or that the weaker would have been condemned exclusively to the occupations of the greatest drudgery and toil. We cannot now inquire how far the existing difference of organization between women and men justifies the withholding from the one enjoyments, and subjecting that one to privations greater than those experienced by the other. The difficulty would certainly be to decide, *which* of the parties should receive the greater enjoyments, *which* should bear the greater privations, the capabilities of both for happiness being equal. All that is wanting for our present purpose is the fact, that this difference of organization between men and women is actually used as a justification of withholding from women in general, and from wives in particular, the same means that men possess of making their talents and faculties—whatever they may be—available to happiness; is used as an argument for subjecting them with inferior powers, whether natural or factitiously produced, to greater pains and privations than men suffer. It will not then, it is to be hoped, be any longer insisted on, that difference of organization between women and men tends to make more gentle, or to render more endurable to women, as wives or otherwise, the despotic control of men over them, than such control would be if exercised by men over their fellow men. The general

98   *If Interests were involved, the Assumption* [Part II.

effect of difference of organization is to decrease the sympathy and render more unfeeling and capricious the control; the alleviation from sexual sympathy being, particularly in the forced state of marriage, partial and trifling in the extreme.

To crown with absurdity the pretensions of men as to their promoting the happiness of their wives equally with their own, let us take another view. What says the "Article"? That " the happiness of wives is involved in "that of their husbands:" which must mean, if it mean any thing, that men are inclined to use their power to advance the happiness of their wives as much as their own. What is the reply that men make to this beautiful theory of their more than disinterested use of power? The very first use they make of it, is to render themselves despotic! each in his several circle the absolute regulator of the personal freedom, the quantum of enjoyments, and what should be the voluntary actions, of his wife, compelling her, however exalted, to swear or vow unqualified obedience to him however debased. Fit commentary on so horrible a falsehood! To show their desire to promote happiness, they reserve to themselves a power of inflicting misery; misery that stops at no tangible mode of torment, that descends into all the minutiæ of thoughts, looks, and inclinations; an inquisition, a familiar, ever present—at every moment that he chooses to be present—from which the victim has no retreat, hopeless as the grave. Suppose that two men, remote from civilization, met each other for the first time, and that one of them happening to be stronger than the other, swore to him that he regarded his happiness as involved in his, as identified with it, and that it was therefore highly unreasonable and superfluous for him, the weaker, to have any will of his own, any control over his own actions; that the care of all such regulation should be taken off his hands, and he, the stronger, would regulate his actions, allot his enjoyments, and allow him liberty of motion when he thought it useful for him; that the weaker had only to swear unlimited obedience to him, and his happiness would be altogether complete, *more safe than if in his own weak keeping*. Would such a man, though strong, be regarded as any thing less than mad? To prove that he considers the interest of his fellow-creature the same as his own, he makes him his slave! Thus with respect to women, to wives—usurping or retaining the unlimited power to do ill, to inflict misery, is an unanswerable demonstration of the inclination to do good, to promote happiness! Away with such stupid, such vile hypocrisy! " By their fruits ye shall know them." Suppose that women asserted that the happiness of men was necessarily involved in theirs: suppose they happened to have been stronger than men, and consequently had the power of proving by their actions that they really sought the happiness of men, say their husbands, as much as their own; suppose the first use women made of this power was to invest themselves with despotic control over the personal liberty, pleasures, actions, and even inclinations of their husbands, instead of guiding them by reason and sympathy, permitting their husbands to have no control over theirs; suppose they said, " man does nothing " for the race; the pain and trouble of forming their bodies " and minds are exclusively ours; why therefore should " man's will oppose itself to ours? let the creature work " under our control, and to us individually and to our de- " sires and caprices *vow* obedience :" who amongst men, who amongst rational beings, would not exclaim that such conduct, so utterly at variance with their professions, was an incontestible proof of the utter want of reason and benevolence in the minds of women, however indisputable might be their possession of superior brute force? Who would not exclaim that the pretence that the interest of men was involved in theirs and could not be separated from it, was by their own act utterly belied? for if the interests were identical, what could be gained by either party by reserving the power of control over the actions of the other? subjection to such controlling power being itself one of the greatest sources of human helplessness and misery. The mere reserving the use of the exercise of such a power at will is a demonstration, that, in the opinion of those reserving it, there necessarily must arise occasions when views of interest of the parties must differ, and when of course the interests of the subjected party must in the opinion of that party suffer. If such would be the absurdity of the pretence, if set up by women, supposing them stronger than men, of a belief in identity of interest if coupled with the assumption of uncontrolled power over the actions of men; why is the absurdity the less on the part of men, being in effect stronger, when they affect that the interests of women are involved in theirs, or identified with them, and still retain despotic power over their conduct?

Nothing therefore can be more impertinent, nothing can be more monstrous, than the pretence that the happiness of wives is involved in that of their husbands, meaning that husbands must necessarily use power to increase their wives' happiness as much as their own. Uncontrolled power necessarily hardens the heart and destroys sympathy for those subjected to it: nor are husbands any exception to this universal law of moral nature. Until man can himself be happy under the same thraldom and domestic confinement to which woman, particularly in marriage, and all her actions are by him subjected, it is the very wantonness of insult to affirm that he consults her happiness as much as his own, while he subjects her to a domination from which his own nature would revolt. The broad undeniable fact that happiness, that is to say *pleasures* constituting the items of happiness, are not by him permitted to be enjoyed by woman to an equal extent with himself, liable to the same restraints, legal, moral, and domestic, and no more than those imposed on himself, must for ever silence the hypocritical pretext that man must necessarily make use of power, in marriage, to render woman as happy as himself, or as happy as she would, possessing the same power, endeavour to make herself.

No person of candour will object to these statements, that a great deal of happiness is in point of fact enjoyed by some individuals, even of the oppressed and degraded party, in marriage, notwithstanding the despotic power possessed by the stronger party. There is no system of slavery ever so brutal that is not capable of being modified in practice by accidental circumstances and individual temperament. The charms of real reciprocal spontaneous esteem, the charms of confidence, are so great, that no baleful institutions can utterly banish them from human life. The wisest of those of the despots, in whom kindly dispositions have been, from whatever fortuitous combination of circumstances, developed, will be those who cultivate the most this source of happiness, in preference to the vulgar pleasure of arbitrary command.

Needs there more in proof of this than an appeal to every reader who has observed the domestic economy of his married acquaintances? Is not the happiness of the parties always in direct proportion to the degree in which the pleasures of persuasion, sympathy, equality of rights and enjoyments, are permitted to supersede the use of the repelling power of arbitrary command? The wife, under existing arrangements, deprived from infancy of freedom and knowledge, and thence of the opportunities of acquiring the habits of judgement and self-control, brought up in habits of submission to unnatural restraints and of blind obedience to arbitrary commands, yoked by an execrable forced vow of superstition to be the voluntary slave of her husband's lusts and caprices; the helpless creature of the vicious system necessarily regards in the husband any relaxation of the rights of supremacy as tokens of peculiar goodness on the part of a master, and perhaps enjoys, as far as her limited mental improvement will permit her to enjoy, something approaching to the pleasures of the intercourse of equals. From the nature of the motives, pecuniary, ambitious, temporary animal appetency of old dotards and young fools, that lead to those indissoluble, and for that reason alone mostly wretched, yokings together, called marriages, in the contracting of which, mutual esteem and affection, which should—in order to promote happiness—be the *only* motives, are looked upon as romantic or ridiculous; it were preposterous to expect that husbands, having uncontrolled power, will not use it ordinarily for their own immediate and exclusive apparent advantage. Women submit to be ordered in every thing, partly from compulsion, partly from pernicious notions of duty, from the same motives that slaves, under all other systems in all parts of the world, submit to their masters. But as the system of slavery in all its modifications is radically unjust, producing an almost equal crop of vice and misery in the master and the slave, it is impossible that passive acquiescence can ever be produced in the minds of slaves, except at the expense of rooting out of them all just notions of morals and all traces of intelligence. If reduced to obey blindly like sheep to the voice of the shepherd, the dog being kept only in terror, and seldom, if ever, biting them, their intellect, their sympathies must be reduced to the level of the sheep, and their happiness to their level, that of eating—sheep need no drink—when and where their masters appoint, and being banqueted upon whenever the caprice of the master judges them worth his enjoyment. Such is one of the many curses of slavery, that it can never procure the submission, not to say the contentment, but at the expense of the utter degradation, of the slave. So is it with the ordinary run of obedient wives. But such models of sheepish, unrepining, unsuspecting, obedience are happily but very rare. " One law " of enjoyment, one law of freedom for the weak, another " for the strong; despotic power exercised by the one, blind " obedience exacted from the other;" such absurdities compel the most stupid to occasional thought; their application in practice, to occasional counter-action. The consequence is, in defect of strength or legal protection, the usual expedients of the slave, cunning and falsehood, are resorted to by wives, and conjoined with ignorance, envies, jealousies and petty malignity, they produce such vexations to the master, as well as to others, as in some measure to retaliate on his head the iniquity, the folly, of his despotism. Where the horror of the system of despotism of the stronger party in marriage is most tremendous, is, in the not unfrequent case, where a woman superior in talents, in virtue, or in both, is bound down in hated obedience to a fool or a vicious wretch, who exercises his power with the more brutality, from the suspicion of his inferiority, from the dread of being looked down upon by the male brutes, his brethren, around him, as compromising by his conduct their claims to supremacy. Those superior women only who have endured the real, not the fabled, hell of such a situation, can adequately paint its horrors; those whose miseries death has not shrouded in their graves! Were the supremacy sought after, that of benevolence and wisdom in a free course of equal competition for mutual influence between men and women living together in marriage, of equal liberty of developement to both, of command to neither, such a supremacy would not be envied to men: wherever they were superior in merit to women living with them in marriage, such supremacy would attend them without envy, without fear Not such is the supremacy they aim at: it is that of the wolf, of force and terror; vile substitute for benevolent persuasion!

The deductions then to be made from the natural abuse of despotic power, in favor of the few cases where peculiarly favorable circumstances overrule its malignant tendencies, and where an approach to an apparent equality of rights and duties leads to an approach to that complete, now unknown, happiness, which perfect equality of intercourse between two individuals bound to each other by sympathy and friendship might produce, are perfectly insignificant. The general rule of isolated breeding establishments, called married life, being now distraction and dissipation on the part of the stronger party, and uncomplaining but unenjoying endurance on the side of the weaker, those few women who are *allowed* by their masters to enjoy, during permission, a *semblance* of equality, which all ought to enjoy without permission, not in semblance but in reality, are looked up to as highly favored beings, whose hearts ought to overflow with gratitude to their masters (for knowing their own interest and making themselves happy); just as the slaves in the West Indies or the southern provinces of the *Free* United States of North America, who have never during their lives been tortured with the whip, are looked upon by their ignorant and degraded fellow-slaves and by their more wicked masters as *extremely fortunate beings*, to be envied by all of their class who are the daily and hourly victims of a hideous system of bodily and mental torture and terror, which forces down below the level of humanity, as to improvement and capability of enjoyment, nine tenths of a community, in order to imbue to the utmost possible degree the remaining tenth with the unsocial vices of cruelty, revenge, suspicion, and sensuality. The untormented slave and the permitted wife may be *comparatively* fortunate: happy they cannot be, till the power of the whip and all other despotic and unequal restraints are taken out of the hands of the wretched masters of each.

The few intelligent and benevolent men who are clear-sighted enough to see their interest in refraining from the use of an odious power of making their fellow-creatures wretched, admit the uselessness of such power to *good* purposes. Why is therefore this pestiferous power to oppress retained? Not by the wise for good, but by the ignorant and brutal for *bad* purposes; to save them the trouble of cultivating their intellectual powers, of learning the art of persuading, of convincing the understanding of their equals, of influencing by the cultivation of sympathy and benevolence! To save such troublesome, such unmanly operations, the brute, though possessing superior strength and affecting the self complacency of superior knowledge,—means abundantly sufficient, if not more than sufficient for all purposes of useful influence,—seizes on the *power to command;* and from that moment seals his own misery, as far as dependent on his connexion in marriage, with the degradation of his slave. If this power of command, not necessary for any useful purposes, not used by the good, is still retained, what does it prove? That it is retained for bad purposes, for gratifying the lust of domination of the stronger over the weaker, for securing to the stronger all those exclusive means of happiness which he may think fit to reserve to himself, for gratifying him with the vicious pleasure of holding the destinies, the happiness or misery of another human being, at his absolute and unaccountable will, that he may be enabled, if so inclined, to exercise all the passions of a fiend on his caged victim, to whom death, or his destruction, is the only refuge from his persecution; all human aid, all human sympathy barred out. Despotism is a power which will never be accepted of by the wise and good, which can be sought for by the ignorant and the wicked alone. Man wishes the happiness of woman living with him in marriage equally with his own; and still retains this desolating power! Unfeeling, insulting hypocrite! till, *in order to add to your own happiness,* you yield similar power to any fellow-creature over your own actions and all your means of enjoyment! then, and not till then, will your pretensions be believed.

Is it necessary to say more? The "Article" asserts that "the happiness of wives is involved in that of their "husbands." I have shown, by facts, that this assertion is a most glaring and pernicious falsehood; that men do on the contrary wantonly trample on the happiness of women living with them in marriage, by assuming and exercising uncontrolled power, and guarantying to each other this uncontrolled power, by what they call laws, over the actions and all the means of happiness of their wives.

The "Article" asserts, "therefore, political rights are "superfluous to women, their happiness being so impar-"tially guarded by men without them."

I assert, " therefore, all women, and particularly women living with men in marriage and unavoidably controlled by their superior strength, having been reduced, by the want of political rights, to a state of helplessness, slavery, and of consequent unequal enjoyments, pains, and privations, they are *more in need* of political rights than any other portion of human beings, to gain some chance of emerging from this state."

Thus have we gone through all the different classes of that half of the human race whom the "Article", under the guise of philosophy, would exclude from political rights, under the false pretext of the superfluity of such rights to their happiness. If notwithstanding the want of these higher rights, women were, in point of fact, every where in possession of the minor, civil and domestic, rights, of equal chances of happiness according to their talents, and liable to equal, and not superior, pains and penalties in case of violating equal duties; if no sexual system of morality had been in consequence of this fatal exclusion established, by means of which man has made his share of morality to consist of activity and enjoyment, and woman's to consist of passive endurance and submission; *then*, with some show of plausibility might it be asserted, " wo-"men have already all the means of improvement and " happiness in proportion to their talents open to them that "men possess, all that political rights could give them ; why " therefore claim that which may be troublesome and ex-" cite envy, but which cannot be beneficial to them ?" Under such circumstances, such a sophism might be endurable, and might be calmly combated, without exciting those profound feelings of indignation and contempt which the hypocritical cruelty of the falsehood engenders, that asserts that man does in fact use his exclusive power as fully and impartially in promoting the happiness of woman as his own.

First, we have shown that the reason the "Article" gives for excluding *all* women from political rights applies, by the admission of the "Article" itself, to but a part of women, to wives and daughters alone. Therefore, in all fairness, an exception should have been made by the "Article" in favor of those women whose interests it admitted were not involved in those of any other individuals exercising political rights. No such exception is, however, made by the "Article": *all* are indiscriminately excluded, because *some* are virtually represented. Those classes of women, having neither fathers nor husbands, not excluded by the reasoning, but excluded by the despotism, of the "Article," are, all young women not having fathers, or leaving their fathers' establishment, till they become married; all women who never marry; all widows. It has been shown that these three numerous classes of women, partly from natural causes, chiefly from partial male legislation excluding them from all means of unfolding their faculties, or of rendering those faculties when unfolded subservient to their happiness, by surrounding them with exclusions of law, superstition, and opinion, are at the same time the most unprotected and the most helpless of the human race, much more so than any classes of men, and that of course their claim to political rights is, on the principles of the "Article," much more cogent than that of any other portion of mankind. These three classes, not noticed by the comprehensive exclusiveness of the "Article," being disposed of; the two classes named as having their interests sufficiently represented by the votes of assignable individuals, namely husbands and fathers, are next considered. The hardiness of the insinuation that fathers are in the habit of using their indirect but not less efficient power and their means of happiness to promote the enjoyments of their adult daughters equally with their own, is brought to light and exposed. From dissimilarity of pursuit and want of sympathy with daughters, from similarity of pursuit and greater sympathy with sons, to whom nevertheless political rights are granted, from the admissions of law, and above all from the glaring and hourly experience of the restraints from freedom and useful pleasures, and exposure to pain and privations, to which adult daughters are subjected equally with young children of both sexes, the futility of the pretence that the interests of daughters are involved in those of their fathers, is demonstrated. The case of the most numerous portion of women, those who enter into such engagements as the laws, made by men, have fabricated for them, to live with men for the purpose of rearing families, under the name of wives, is last inquired into. Over this most numerous and every where degraded class of human beings, in addition to the indirect influence which fathers exercise over their daughters in spite of the inefficient rights which they, in common with adult sons, possess, men have every where invested themselves with *despotic power*, and have, by all the arts of excluding knowledge, of peculiar training, and of superstition, formed the minds as well as the bodies of their victims to such impotence, that they either voluntarily spring forward to meet the yoke and *vow* themselves slaves, or submit in sullen apathy to their fate; reducing to the very lowest term the happiness that might be derived to both parties from an equal intercourse of the sexes equally improved and equally independent of each other's caprices. The peculiar liability of wives to oppression more than even daughters, and with no increase of power in the hands of the husband over and above that possessed by fathers, was pointed out. It arises from the isolation of every wife living alone and unsupported under the roof of a being stronger than herself; while adult daughters have almost always the sympathy and support of each other, of their mother, and occasionally of their brothers; from all which wives are from their situation mostly excluded. Inferior in strength, inferior in knowledge, dependent for the supply of the necessaries, not to speak of the comforts, of life, on the caprices of the man with whom she lives; with such immense means of indirect influence in his hands to render his wife subservient to his will, one is apt to wonder at that savage and preposterous lust of power which could lead men possessing such fearful advantages, each over his caged, alternate plaything and tool, to clothe themselves with open and undisguised despotic license of capricious command. Was not the solid power of making wretched and of laughing at appeals, under such circumstances, to law, for protection, even were such appeals to law allowed, sufficient for men, without the insulting display of such power, without investing themselves with a superfluous legal right to exercise oppression at their pleasure? Such is the fatal use which man has made of his exclusive possession of political rights over the weaker half of his race, women, and particularly over those women whom he calls wives; and such are the fatal degradation and misery to which women are reduced by the loss of such rights! The alleviation that might be produced to women in the exercise of this odious power to make wretched, from the sexual dependence of husbands on their wives, was investigated; and it was shown that not only was this dependence mutual and therefore neutralized, but the dependence of man in this respect was both from law, practice, and morals, a mere farce in marriage, the contravention attended with no evil; while with respect to woman the dependence was real, and the contravention attended with consequences legal, practical, and moral, unrelentingly enforced, and next in severity to the loss of existence. The alienation, almost amounting to antipathy, instead of increased sympathy, arising from a difference of organization between all animals, where sexual feelings are not immediately concerned, was pointed out. The absolute impossibility also was urged of any individual, vested with despotic power over another, whether of the same or a different sex, being capable, if ever so well inclined, of using such power as effectually to promote the happiness of that other as that individual could do by personal use of the same power. The only and the real circumstances that modify man's domination over woman are, the superfluous uselessness of a brutal exercise of power from the utter abjectness and submission of the trained and ignorant slave, as well as the necessity of keeping his slave in a state of apparent cheerfulness, that his commands may be obeyed with more alacrity, and that his hours of condescending dalliance may be rendered more attractive. The pleasures of all sorts, those of the senses, intellectual, moral, particularly those of social intercourse and personal freedom, which men enjoy exclusively, and from which they debar their wives, were pointed out; and both from the unqualified powers which they have assumed, and the mode in which they exercise those powers, their inclination to make their wives as happy as themselves, to regard the interests of their wives as involved in theirs, appeared a matter of derision. The systematic exclusion of women from all useful knowledge in education and after-life, the horrible system of sexual, pretended morals, making the very same actions indifferent or meritorious, and always unpunished, in the stronger party, which are called vicious, sinful, and always cruelly punished, in the weaker party, and the immoral vow which superstition ultimately exacts from creatures so prepared, to devote themselves blindly obedient to all the unhallowed lusts and caprices of the men, whoever they may be, that marry them, were all noticed and put forward as unanswerable illustrations of the effects of vesting the political rights of one half the human race in the keeping of the other half. While man is man, he will never take the *trouble* of depriving any of his fellow-creatures of their political rights, without a dishonest view, without a motive of advantage to himself. The very same reason that leads those possessing political power to exclude any of their fellow-men from the equal possession of political rights, is that which leads them to exclude all women; namely, the short-sighted desire of ignorance and self-will, of being happy at their expense.

Is it not then abundantly demonstrated that no statement ever laid down by philosopher was more entirely false, more at variance with the nature of the human mind and with the well-known daily course of action of all men, than that which asserts that the interests of women, say of daughters and wives, are "involved in the interests of men," namely, of fathers and husbands?

Were this the space to enter fully into the situation of women—a task that may be undertaken hereafter, should life and health permit—were we not here limited to the refutation of a particular and novel pretence set up for the eternal exclusion of one half the human race from political rights (involving as they do all other sources of happiness), a comparative sketch might be given of the state of married women in different countries, from which it would appear that the happiness of the male as well as the female, and of the whole of society, is in a direct ratio to an approach to an equality of cultivation and improvement, of rights and duties, between husbands and wives; the extreme of slavery being the most wretched, the nearest approach to equal liberty and equal restraint the most happy, to all parties.

PART II.

———

QUESTION II.—*If this involving of the interests of women in those of men do exist, is it a sufficient cause, or any reason at all, why either of the parties, men or women, with interests so identified, should therefore be deprived of civil or political rights?*

TOPICS OF QUESTION II.

The effect of the exercise of political rights by women on the happiness of *men* is superfluous and irrelevant to the argument: the question is as to its effect on the happiness of *women* . page 118

Strength is no title to superior happiness 120

Two grand reasons for which political rights are valuable; first, to obtain and secure civil and domestic rights, or security of person and property; second, as the most efficient means of improving the intellectual and social powers 121

The second of these objects, the improvement of the intellectual and social powers, can only be attained by the personal exercise of political rights: this object peculiarly desirable for women, to counteract the tendency of their habits 124

Would the *exclusive* exercise of political rights be attended with the least evil, if placed in the hands of men or women? . . 126

Reasons in favor of the exclusive exercise by women . . 127

Reasons in favor of the exclusive exercise by men . . . 128

The most important of the qualifications for making useful public regulations—viz. sympathy with those to be affected by the regulations, or moral aptitude—would be more certainly exerted in women, if sole legislators, than in men 129

Intellectual aptitude for legislation, or appropriate knowledge, would be as great in exclusive female, as in exclusive male, legislators 135

Talent for original discovery, or genius, not requisite in legislators 137

Topics of Question the Second. 115

Doubtful whether less appropriate active talent for legislation would be found in women than in men 139

Moral aptitude, or probity, in legislation, of more importance than intelligence and activity combined 146

Exercise of political rights, is a source not only of innocent, but of useful gratification 148

Individual competition banishes sympathy 149

Summary of argument against exclusions, even on the hypothesis of an identity, or involving, of interests 150

Two great stages of human improvement; the one, the simple removal of restraints, the cessation of the empire of force and fraud; the other, the raising of the superstructure of human happiness. In the co-operation of large numbers for common and equal enjoyment, alone, can the latter, the science of human happiness, be practically as well as theoretically pursued 151

PART II.

QUESTION II.—*If this involving of the interests of women in those of men do exist, is it a sufficient cause, or any reason at all, why either of the parties, men or women, with interests so identified, should therefore be deprived of civil or political rights?*

THE basis of the theory on which the "Article" founds the propriety of the political slavery of women, followed, as a necessary consequence and as a matter of fact, by their civil and domestic slavery, thus swept away, we come to the second question, which it is curious and useful to solve, though not absolutely requisite to the purpose in hand. The only reason the "Article" gives for the exclusion of women from political rights being founded on an assumption of facts shown to be utterly false, the removal of the exclusion should follow as a matter of course. But the unsoundness of this basis of exclusion is not more flagrant than are the inferences which are deduced from it, *even if the basis were founded on truth.* Let us inquire then, supposing that the interests of men and women were so involved in each other, that the one possessing power necessarily used it impartially for the equal happiness of both, would that be a sufficient reason for excluding either party, or in particular for excluding women, from the equal participation in political as well as in all other rights, or means of happiness, with the other, the male half of the species? If the inference in favor of exclusion from the involving of interests, can be demonstrated a mere vulgar impertinence, adopted at random, without any research into facts or consequences, then the equal claim of all the adult portion of the human race to political rights, founded on their claim to equal happiness, from the fact of their equal capacity to enjoy it, must at once stand admitted. For though we cannot here enter into the general question of excluding women from the same means of developing their powers, and making them available to their happiness, that men possess; though we cannot here refute the numerous insipidities and brutalities of pretended statement and pretended reasoning, put forward by the ignorance and intoxication of men, generated by the daily use of despotic power, in support of their self-degrading and self-tormenting usurpations; although we cannot here open out the perspective of intelligence, beneficence, and happiness which would result equally to both sexes from the banishment of sexual morals, sexual laws, and from the establishment of equal education, equal rights and duties, equal justice in every particular between women and men;—yet will the presumption be almost irresistible, that as the philosophy of the "Article" itself has rejected all these worn-out follies, by not condescending to make use of them, and seeking for a new basis on which to continue and perpetuate the old exclusions of half the human race; nay, as the general reasoning of the "Article" includes all sentient rational adults in the benefits of self-government, and passes by women along with children on the mere plea of a supposed *super-*

fluousness of such rights to the protection of their interests, (the interests of such creatures being, as the "Article" supposes, sufficiently promoted by a state of ignorance and slavery, beyond which state of exquisite well-being they cannot possibly have any wishes!) not from any pretended evils put forward as likely to arise from their exercise of political rights, this superfluousness being shown not to exist,—it will follow that all those at least who are convinced by the general reasoning of the "Article," of the necessity of self-government to promote and protect the happiness of men, belonging to the stronger half of the race, against the attacks of their fellow-men, will for a stronger reason admit the necessity of self-government to promote and protect the happiness of women, the weaker half of the race, against the attacks of men, the stronger half; men always possessing, individual for individual, the physical power to oppress. Without exclusions, inferiority of strength or intelligence must be attended with inferiority of happiness. Why aggravate by exclusions the inevitable operation of such physical sources of misery, or at least of diminished chances of happiness?

Is it then true that, provided the interests of women are involved in those of men, they ought to be, in order to promote their happiness, excluded from the exercise of political rights?

It is not necessary here to discuss whether it would promote the happiness of *men* that women should under such circumstances enjoy political rights. Women are one half the human race, and as much entitled to happiness on their own account, for their own sakes, as men. Just as necessary would it be to inquire whether the possession of political rights by men would tend to promote the happiness of women. The happiness of every individual, and of course of all classes, of the human race, ought to be promoted for the sake of such individual or individuals, and not in subserviency to the happiness of any other individuals or classes whatever. When every individual is made happy, the happiness of the whole is promoted. The mountebank jargon of a "public good" distinct from the good of the individual members of society, will lead astray the human mind no more. It will be found that no person or persons can promote their real happiness, looking comprehensively into all the results of their actions, by any line of conduct which is incompatible with the happiness of others; that is to say, which detracts more from their happiness than it adds to that of the agent or agents. It is incumbent on those disapproving of any given line of conduct in others, to show, not only that such line of conduct is absolutely indifferent to them, that it does *not add* to their happiness,—but to point out how it interferes with, how it *lessens,* their happiness: that demonstrated, it will cease to be the interest of the agent to pursue such injurious conduct, because the necessary re-actions of selfishness of others and of their sympathy with the injured will more than counterbalance the apparent individual immediate gain. The interests therefore of all human beings, their real comprehensive interests, calculating all the consequences of their actions and pursuing that which will promote preponderant good, thus reconciling individual with general welfare, ought to be pursued for all, and for all classes; the interests of women for their own sakes, the interests of men for theirs. What reason can men give, what reason can any individuals of the human race give, that their happiness should be promoted, which cannot be equally given by any other individuals, by women? They live, and are capable of happiness without detracting a greater portion of happiness from others than that which they enjoy or may be made to enjoy. This is the common, the only, and the sufficient title to happiness of all the individuals of the human race. The title of man cannot reside in his possession of superior strength, because that cannot increase his sensual and intellectual capabilities of happiness; nor if exerted in opposition to reason, to a comprehensive survey of the consequences of his actions, will it add to his happiness. If strength be the superior title to happiness, let the knowledge and skill of man be employed in adding to the pleasurable sensations of horses, elephants, and all stronger animals. If strength be the title to happiness, let all such qualifications for voters as the capacity to read and write, or any *indirect* means to insure intellectual aptitude, be abolished; and let the simple test for the exercise of political rights, both by men and women, be the capacity of carrying 300 lbs. weight. Superior strength, superior intelligence, are amongst the means of rendering this equal title to happiness more available, but cannot constitute the title: on the contrary, superior strength and intelligence would, under the guidance of a more enlarged self-interest, display themselves in compensating to the weaker and less intelligent for their want of happiness from these sources, by the practice of beneficence, the most productive mode of disposing of superfluous energies, instead of employing them in vulgar exclusions, engendering vice and misery to both parties, to those who exclude and to those who are excluded.

We maintain then that, "supposing the interests of

men and women to be so involved in each other, that the advancement of one is necessarily followed by that of the other, that power given to one, particularly political power, is necessarily used impartially for the advantage of both,—it would no more follow that women should, than that men should, be on that account excluded from the exercise of political rights."

For what reasons are political rights claimed by men? For two leading reasons. First, because without them they could never enjoy the civil rights of property and person, or if by chance they obtained possession of any of these civil rights, they could not have a moment's security in the enjoyment of them, without the guarantee of their own power through representatives under their control for the continuance of them. The second reason, though almost entirely overlooked, is scarcely secondary in importance to the first. It is, that the exercise of political rights affords the best opportunity for the exercise of the intellectual powers and enlargement of the sympathies of human beings, leading their attention out of themselves, to matters in which numbers of their fellow creatures, to an indefinite extent besides themselves, are interested.

Now supposing that the interests of men and women were so mysteriously involved in each other, that either party exercising political rights would necessarily promote the civil rights and consequently the happiness of the other equally with their own; as far as civil rights are concerned, this might be a good reason for indifference in the party excluded from political rights as to the possession of them; but it could be no reason at all as to the loss of the second benefit to be derived from the exercise of such political rights. The one party exercising political rights from which the other was excluded, could not by any means impart to that other the exercise of the intellectual powers, and that enlargement of sympathy, that interest in the affairs of numbers mixed with our own, which distinguishes the benevolent from the selfish. This vice of character, want of comprehensive views, want of interest in any thing out of themselves or of their own little domestic circle,—the necessary result of the state of barbarous exclusion, of domestic imprisonment, in which women have been kept,—can never be cured by the enjoyment by any others than themselves of those opportunities for unfolding their powers, which enlarged social, including political, interests, can alone create. Had the party possessing political power used it with ever so much impartiality, had the civil rights and duties, privations and punishments of women for the same offences, been the same as those of men, still would all this—so flagrantly contrary to the actual result of their exclusion—be no justification whatever of the withholding from them political rights. Without them they can never have enlargement of mind, they can never have expansive benevolence; because without them they can never pass through those *incidents* which are necessary to the unfolding of such qualities. Look to the state of the minds of men in any part of the world excluded from political rights, though enjoying the power of locomotion and equal in point of civil rights (if such state of things any where exist) to their neighbours, and you will find either eternal discontent or an abjectness of mind and want of benevolence on the part of the excluded, which denotes the source from which the vice of their characters proceeds. How much more must this be the case with women shut out from those transactions and incidents of busy life which afford exercise, the means of developement, to the human powers!

Here then is an effect to be produced, the developement of character, of intelligence and benevolence, by the exercise of political rights, which the "Article" has entirely overlooked. The effect which the "Article" insinuated to be substantially effected notwithstanding the exclusion of women from political rights, namely, the equal participation in happiness with men, has been shown to be flagrantly false. And in addition to this evil comes another as great, or only secondary to it in importance,—want of enlargement of mind, of formation of character, which is equally sacrificed. In fact, without an enlargement of mind and benevolence, the capacity would be wanting for enjoying in the highest degree those means of happiness which the possession of equal civil rights, supposed to be conceded by men, would put into women's hands. Were the position therefore of the "Article" true as to the flimsy pretext of an identity or an involving of interests—to be only laughed at, if it were not, for its hypocritical malignity and pernicious effects in misery, to be execrated—the secondary evil here pointed out would remain an eternal bar to the exclusion of any of the adult portion of the human race from the exercise of political power, as a means of improvement. From the casualties of gestation, women are necessarily, at least for a considerable portion of their time, more stationary and confined than men, and more inclined to mere local and personal sympathies. To counteract then this tendency of their physical situation to confined views and feelings, a *greater* necessity than in the case of men, rather than a less, exists, that opportunities should be afforded them for overcoming this tendency to selfishness, and for cultivating the enlarged and benevolent affections. The cultivation of these on a large scale never makes the enjoyment of them less dear on a scale more confined, but clears such enjoyment of its degrading weaknesses, and heightens the sensual, and confined sympathetic, pleasures, by association. Is the *man* who is remarkable for comprehensive benevolence less apt on that account to indulge in kindness towards those with whom he is immediately connected? Why then a woman? Is *man* less an object of love to woman, less capable of feeling and inspiring love, because he is intelligent and benevolent? because he rejoices in the happiness of all who smile upon or around him? Why then should woman, in consequence of the same enlarged sympathies and comprehensiveness of mind, be less an object of love to man, be less likely to increase her own enjoyments? These opportunities for enlargement of character, can never be afforded but by possessing an influence in public affairs, in matters of public interest; for where influence is excluded, interest cannot be felt, influence, not of mere power or command nor of the corruptive class, but influence arising from the exercise of the understanding. How doubly vain therefore is the hollow pretext put forward by the "Article," of excluding women from political rights on account of the involving of their interests with those of men! Will enlargement of mind and benevolence tend less to their happiness than to that of men? will it tend less to the happiness of those with whom they associate? Can these qualities be unfolded in man or woman if opportunities are not given for their developement? How but by discussing and influencing the affairs in which numbers, sometimes to the whole extent of all mankind, are concerned, and in which the individual is connected with and merged in the general interest, can such enlargement and such benevolence be produced? Will the exercise of handicraft trades by men make women expert in such trades? As little can the exercise of the intellectual powers or of the sympathetic affections by men unfold those qualities in women, shut out from a participation in the incidents necessary to unfold them. Will reading, or hearing read, the description of manual operations, without practice and without benefit to be derived from the practice, ever make any human beings expert in such operations? As little will exhortations to enlargement of mind and to culture of social feelings avail in producing them, where the fields for the exercise, and the motives to the exercise, of them, are withheld. Can we expect grapes from thorns? If we really wish that women should participate in that enlargement of mind and benevolence of which we vainly boast, but do not possess, as our actions demonstrate, wherefore withhold from them the means of cultivating such qualities? Be consistent, men! Ye stronger half of the race, be at length rational! Three or four thousand years have worn threadbare your vile cloak of hypocrisy. Even women, your poor, weak, contented slaves, at whose impotence of penetration, the result of your vile exclusions you have been accustomed to laugh, begin to see through it and to shudder at the loathsomeness beneath. Cast aside this tattered cloak before it leaves you naked and exposed. Clothe yourselves with the new garments of sincerity. Be rational human beings, not mere male sexual creatures. Cast aside the ferocious brute of your nature: give up the pleasures of the brute, those of mere lust and command, for the pleasures of the rational being. So shall you enjoy the love of your *equals*, enlightened, benevolent, graceful, like yourselves, founded on an appreciation of your real merits: so shall you be happy. For the intercourse of the *bought* prostitute, or of the *commanded* household slave, you shall have full and equal participation in the compounded and associated pleasures of sense, intellect and benevolence. To the highest enjoyments of which your nature is susceptible, there is no shorter road than the simple road of equal justice.

Suppose it to be conceded, then, to the "Article", that the interests of men and women are so involved in each other, that political power possessed by the one must be impartially used for the benefit of both. The question still remains to be solved: To which of the two would it be most useful, most tending to preponderant good—to which of the two, to women or to men, seeing that the happiness of both would be effectually promoted by the exercise of power in the hands of either, ought the exercise of political rights to be confined?

No one will for a moment suppose that by entering into this discussion, to which the hardihood of our adversary compels us, we entertain the most distant notion of the propriety of investing either half of the human race, the stronger or the weaker, with the exclusive power of making regulations affecting the actions, the property, and therefore in every possible way, the happiness of the whole. No one can suppose that the writer of these pages is not an utter enemy to the exclusion from political rights of any one rational adult being of the human race. This premised,

What are the reasons that might be put forth on the part of women, and what those which might be put forth on the part of men, in favor of investing each of them respectively with the exclusive exercise of political power?

In favor of women it might be stated;

> First, that being the weaker party in point of strength, though equally, or more susceptible of pleasure and pain, their happiness would be (as in point of fact it has been) altogether sacrificed, if the power of legislation were thrown into the hands of the stronger party.
>
> Second, that with respect to the interests of the excluded stronger party, for whom as well as for themselves they would be thus called on to legislate, they could not overlook them, because the superior strength of men never would submit to injustice from hands unable to enforce it, and because such knowledge would lead the weaker never wilfully to make any partial, unjust regulations in their own favor. Moreover, as mothers, they would be equally interested in promoting the happiness of their sons as of their daughters.
>
> Third, that as muscular is generally cultivated at the expense of intellectual power, and as women are less adapted to the cultivation of the muscular powers, it is probable that, were the career of intellectual improvement open to them as that of muscular developement is to men, women would excel as much in intelligence as men in strength, and would therefore be better adapted than men to the making of wise laws; while of

all the knowledge of men they would also necessarily avail themselves.

Fourth, that the tendency of the organization of women, from want of equal muscular strength with men, being rather to intellectual and sympathetic pursuits than those of brute force, they would be more apt in legislation to cultivate the arts of persuasion and peace, and to avoid offensive wars, one of the greatest scourges of humanity.

In favor of vesting the exclusive power of making laws in men, it might be stated;

First, that not being liable like women to occasional pain and confinement from the gestation and rearing of children, their undivided and uninterrupted attention might be given to the important concern of making good laws.

Second, that being possessed of superior strength, their laws would carry their own sanction with them, and would be necessarily obeyed and operative.

Third, that men are, in point of fact, the most intelligent of the two portions into which the human race is divided, and therefore the most able to make wise laws.

Fourth, that men are, in point of fact, possessed also of more active talent than women, and therefore more able to go through the mental, as well as bodily, fatigues attendant on legislation.

On a general view of the qualities most indispensable for good legislation, it will be found that the disposition to sympathize with all, and to promote the happiness of all, whom the laws in question are to affect, is by far the most valuable. Without this, the other qualities of superior wisdom, leisure, power, and activity, could be of no use, except by accident; but might be, and most probably would be, converted into the instruments of more extensive mischief than could be produced by the non-possession of them. It is difficult indeed to suppose that real knowledge could long exist on a branch of morals so important as legislation, without leading to the perception of the important truth, that sympathy for the happiness of those for whom laws are made is the most indispensable quality in the makers of laws. The perception of the truth however is one thing, and the yielding to its influence is quite another. The yielding to its influence depends upon the position in which the individual legislators are placed respecting those whose happiness their regulations must affect, such position giving birth to motives which necessarily influence their conduct. But as soon as their knowledge should lead them so to alter their position as to be liable to be influenced by a universal sympathy for the happiness of all for whom they legislate, they would no longer wish to pursue any exclusive ends, nor of course to legislate for those who did not depute them.

We return therefore to the position that the disposition to sympathize with the pains and pleasures, to promote the happiness, of all liable to be affected by laws, is the most useful of the qualities which legislators can possess. Women, as exclusive legislators, would be more apt to possess this quality than men as exclusive legislators. Men, as exclusive legislators, have every where sacrificed not only the interests of one half the race, women; but have also trampled every where on the happiness of as large a portion of their own half of the race, of their fellow-men, as their cunning and power permitted. their short-sighted desires to accomplish. Wherefore? Because, having the co-operation of the superior strength of all *men* in their favor, as against the weaker half, women, they were able without effort and by means of a common supposed interest and universal partnership of injustice, every man in his sphere the despot of every woman, to put aside the claims of the weaker half of the race. Freed from any apprehension on their account, from any fear of union for joint interest between them and the portion of their own sex whose interests they made subservient to what to them appeared to be their own, exclusive male legislators have been enabled to direct their undivided attention to the degradation, to the keeping down of their own sex. Woman, the universal slave of the oppressed as well as of the oppressors amongst men, has been necessarily indifferent to their contests for power, for the right to plunder and torment each other; well aware, from universal experience, that no alleviation would soothe her destiny, however her masters might distribute amongst themselves the powers of mutual annoyance, and too unenlightened to perceive, in the distance, the universal recovery of the rights of women, as a consequence of that improvement of reason in opposition to brute force which must lay the foundation of the equal rights of men. Even this distant gleam of hope, it is true, the philosophical "Article on Government" coldly extinguishes, by assuring women that philosophy, regarding their happiness as involved in that of men, deems political rights superfluous to them: but the impotence of such an extinguisher has, it is hoped, been long ago made apparent.

Let it not be supposed that so undeserved a compliment is meant to be paid to the comprehensiveness of view of exclusive male legislators, as to suppose that they planned their regulations of oppression with a distant foresight of these complicated results. They were for the most part too much of brutes to foresee them, guided by momentary passions with a view to their own apparent immediate interest. It is not the less true, however, that such results, foreseen by them or not, have every where accrued from the indulgence in passions every where excited by a similarity of circumstances.

True to the principles of *governing by division*, exclusive male legislators, disembarrassing themselves of one half the race by a universal, mutually conceded, and mutually supported league to oppress, each in his domain, that weaker, isolated, and divided half, have pursued the same policy towards their own sex. They have made it the immediate interest of the strongest, the richest, and the most knowing, to join them in oppressing the rest; whence the chaos of miseries which, all over the globe, force, in the hands of men possessing political power, has produced. Is it possible to conceive that legislative power lodged exclusively in the hands of women, without force, the weaker half of the race, could have produced atrocities and wretchedness equal to those with which exclusive male legislation has desolated the globe? Is there no hope that under the exclusive legislation of women, some at least of these palpable and avowed evils would have been obviated or lessened?

There is the strongest ground for hope, amounting

almost to a certainty, that the exclusive legislation of women would have been much more beneficent—less beneficent it is almost impossible to conceive it to be capable of being—than that of men has absolutely been; because the sympathies of women for the whole race, for all those liable to be affected by their regulations, must, from the fact of their inferior physical strength, have been much more active than those of men, and much more inclined to promote impartially the happiness of all. Our inclinations arise from our relative positions with respect to others, and from the probability of being able to gratify them. Women possessed of exclusive legislative power, having as a body less strength than men, the now supposed excluded half of their species, could not rule them by force. What would be the consequence? They must rule them by persuasion: they must calculate in every thing the effect of their regulations on the feelings, on the real happiness, of men, as much as of women. They could not dispose of one half of their race, as men, from the possession of superior strength, have done, amongst each other, every woman in the community the arbitrary regulator of the destiny of one man, her household slave. They could not so parcel out man into individual slavery as men have actually parcelled out women: superior average strength on the part of men would render so wicked a project of isolation impossible. Unable then to put down and degrade men by force, and thus to put them out of the social scale, they would not be free to turn their undivided attention to the oppression of their own sex, as men have every where done towards theirs. As a counterpoise to the overwhelming physical force of men, they would be under the necessity of dispensing equal justice, according to their notions of justice, amongst all of their own sex. If they attempted to make unequal laws, to oppress any portion of the great ruling community of women, they would find the oppressed portion of women immediately supported by the excluded, and therefore always discontented, half of the race, men. The malcontent women would always have such powerful auxiliaries in men, that women in possession of all the legislative, judicial, and administrative offices of a community (those alone requiring superior physical force excepted) would not venture on oppressing them, as the great majority of men are now every where oppressed by men. If their laws were equal as to their own sex, the now supposed privileged portion of the race, they could not be unequal as to men. Women, constantly feeling their inferiority of strength, would not dare by partial regulations against men to tempt their physical powers of resistance into action. They would be forced from interest to make the most useful regulations their knowledge would permit; otherwise their regulations would remain unrespected, unsubmitted to. These circumstances, in which women as exclusive legislators and administrators would be placed, would as necessarily generate in them a sympathy for the interests of all those, both men and women, over whom their regulations extended, as an opposite set of circumstances have necessarily, and in point of fact, generated a want of sympathy in male legislators for all those, men and women, over whom their regulations have extended. Over women in authority men would always have the effectual restraint of strength and of the dread on the part of their rulers of provoking its exercise. Wherever the complete operation of this salutary restraint is wanting, misrule, as the "Article on Government" has sufficiently illustrated, is certain to ensue. There only where it prevails, can either equal or just laws be expected. Over women as exclusive legislators, though deputed by women alone, this check would be always in constant operation. Over men as exclusive legislators, deputed by men alone, it could never operate but in favor of men. Over women, as exclusive legislators, it operates in favor of both men and women, of the whole of a community. With the whole of a community would women therefore, exclusively legislating, sympathize: with one half only of the community would men, exclusively legislating, sympathize. Which is better therefore—that legislators should sympathize with the half, or the whole of those whose happiness their regulations affect? If with the whole, it would be more wise for the whole race that women than that men should be exclusive legislators, inasmuch as moral aptitude, or an inclination to promote the happiness of the governed, would be more certainly found in women than in men. Were no other boon derived from the exclusive legislation of women, over placing this same exclusive power in the hands of men, the single fact of the interests of women being thereby equally promoted with those of men, as far as disposition is concerned, is quite sufficient to incline the balance in favor of women's exclusive rule as the least pernicious of the two expedients. The degraded half of the race being thereby raised to an equality with the now monopolizing and oppressive half, (the greater portion of that half itself always oppressed,) could never be, by exclusive legislation in the hands of women, not only not more oppressed than it has been by male legislators, but could not be oppressed at all, as far as existing knowledge could guaranty from oppression. Exclusive male legislators have an essential disposition to consult the happiness, at the most, of one half of those (their male constituents) whose interests their regulations affect; while in women the disposition must be to consult the happiness of the whole. Where rulers cannot attain their ends by compulsion, they are necessitated to use the more useful means of reason and persuasion; as in the Non-slave United States of America.

To this add the greater inclination of women, necessarily produced by the incidents of domestic life and of business carried on with beings of superior strength, to regard the interests of men, not only as of equal importance with their own, but even, perhaps, to imbibe so much of the present prejudice in favor of superior strength as habitually to regard the interests of men as rather more important than those of women.

But there are other qualities desirable in legislators besides an inclination to sympathize with the happiness of the governed, otherwise called probity or moral aptitude. These are intellectual aptitude and active talent. Whether would male or female exclusive legislators be more apt to be imbued with these qualities also? It would seem that exclusive female legislators would be on a par with exclusive males as to knowledge or intellectual aptitude, but would, *perhaps*, be inferior as to activity or active talent.

Whether the capability of intellectual improvement exists to a greater degree in the weaker or the stronger half of the human race, or whether, as is more probable, the organical capabilities are equal, on an average, in a given number of both sexes, is a question in our present state of experimental, the only real, knowledge on the subject, quite undecided. The superior capability must be so very small, if inclining to either side, that the solution of the question is quite unimportant to any part of our argument. The difference, if any, can only exist in the aptitude to make discoveries, to extend the bounds of knowledge, or in what is called original genius. That both sexes are equally capable of being taught, of comprehending, appreciating, and making their own all the knowledge accumulated on moral and physical subjects, and judging of that knowledge, similar facilities being afforded to each, the most ample experience has fully evinced. Those circumstances, superadded to organization, on which original genius or the faculty of discovering new truths, or describing or executing works of art in a new and interesting manner, depend, are so delicate and so much out of the control of the ordinary current of education, that until all women are afforded equal chances with men to be operated upon by such circumstances, it is quite idle almost to give a guess as to which half of the race would more excel in genius and discovery. The probability is, that with equal facilities, genius would be equal : for if the greater inclination of men to muscular exertion would distract more of their average attention than of that of women from intellectual pursuits, the attention of those men who applied themselves to such pursuits might be more uninterrupted than that of women, liable to the average distractions of gestation. Let these two circumstances balance each other ; and as far as probabilities previous to absolute experience can lead, it would seem that discoveries might be equally shared by both. But were it otherwise, had experiments been made on the largest scale, were it demonstrated that women, on an average of persons, possessed a less instead of a greater aptitude to genius or discovery than men—what would follow? That they would therefore have less intellectual aptitude *for legislation*, and for the executing of national regulations when made, than men? No such inference would follow.

What are the intellectual qualities wanting in legislators? Would an assembly of legislators formed of all the discoverers of the age on all the branches of physics and morals, be possessed of the most useful qualities for the making of useful national regulations, whether composed of men or women? Discoverers almost always over-estimate the relative importance of the branch of knowledge to which they are attached, and are frequently apt to neglect the acquisition of other branches of knowledge. Now those two defects, which it is so difficult for discoverers to avoid, are just those intellectual defects which would be the most pernicious in legislators. General, not peculiar, knowledge is particularly desirable in legislators. So many elements, no less than the interests of the whole community, of all the individuals of all the classes of which it is composed, enter into every legislative measure, that the absolute neglect of any one branch of knowledge might cause the judgement of the mind so deficient, to err. It is only a mind stored with general knowledge that can have that equal regard for the interests of all, or, though having regard, that can impartially promote the interests of all, which is the first duty of legislators. Again—the mind that can judge calmly of a discovery, that is anxious for every new truth, and anxious also to guard against error in the shape of fancied discovery, that will receive and spread the useful truth to all unshackled minds, is much better calculated to make it useful in legislation than the orginal discoverer. Had the original discoverer the power, he ought not to wish to cause his discovery to be adopted by any other means than those of persuasion. But the legislators with faculties to judge and to persuade, but not equal to original discovery, are exactly those whom it would be the most desirable to convince of the utility of any thing new. Influenced by no fondness for the children of their own genius, they could with the more effect communicate it to others, and cause its adoption when, and not before, it had operated on a mass of minds and made them prepared to receive and diffuse its benefits. If we admit therefore to the fullest extent the monstrous assumption that women are utterly inferior to men in the faculty of invention; since not that faculty, but the faculty of a sound judgement and the acquisition of all ascertained useful knowledge are the intellectual qualities most requisite; and, after moral aptitude, the most useful of all qualities, in legislators; it would still appear that the minds of women would be on that very account better fitted for legislative operations than those of men; were we forced to choose between them, and not to leave the election to all parties, men and women, interested in choosing those, women or men, best adapted to the duties they were called upon to perform. A new project, ever so useful, ought not to be adopted as a legislative measure, until the minds of those whom it was destined to serve, as well as of those through whom it was to be diffused, were prepared to receive it, if not with cordiality at least without antipathy. Now women being by the supposition capable of judging but not of inventing, and it having been shown that, as exclusive legislators, they would be necessarily more inclined to promote the interest of all than men as exclusive legislators, it follows that their intellectual powers would be the best fitted for such operations, and the best directed. What is the wisdom developed by men which women could not acquire? acquire as easily as all those men, the immense majority of that half the race, whom peculiar organization or peculiar circumstances, or both, do not call to the exercise of the higher powers of invention? Of all the knowledge of men women could avail themselves. Of what consequence to those benefited by equal and good laws without being equal they could not be really good; though, being equal, they might still be unjust to all—that the wisdom by which they were made was second-hand? Gold assayed produces the most confidence and is the most useful. Truth addressed to those whose inclination and interest, as well as duty, it is to receive it, will not be long shut out: addressed to women as legislators it would be eminently their interest as well as duty to receive it; the jealousy and envy of rival inventions and counter-schemes would not oppose its reception.

From that species of intellectual power requisite for legislation which experience has proved may, by similar circumstances, be developed equally in women and men, we pass to the third requisite—active talent. It has already been acknowledged that women, as exclusively possessed of political rights, would be deficient in this quality compared with men. But what would be the amount of the deficiency? and of what importance would it be as affecting the general result of useful regulation, compared with the other two qualities, in one of which women were found to have greater, and in the other to have equal aptitude with men?

Inclination to do good, and knowing the means to do

good, or moral and intellectual aptitude for any purpose, are of no practical benefit without that portion of activity which is requisite to perform the necessary acts to accomplish the purpose desired. True that the inclination cannot be very energetic without calling the active talent into exercise. But there are cases, such as those of physical incapacity, as well as mental disease—the want of the *habit* of exertion—which so frequently occur as to justify the separate consideration of appropriate active talent as a third ingredient towards the accomplishment of any continued purpose. Now, that peculiar species of active aptitude which is necessary for the purpose in hand, is rather mental than muscular activity ; not that activity which requires strength, but which requires patience and perseverance. And such is just the species of activity of which women are most possessed, and which the developement of their powers would most surely call forth. Sedentary occupations are disdained by the locomotive propensities, the love of command, of men. Hence all household occupations, all anxious weary watchings, the irritations of which would wear down the stubborn frame of men, are universally thrown by them as drudgeries upon women. To endure privation and wrong, to return contumely with never-tired, never-ending submission, to sympathize with and soothe, the distressed in pains of mind or body, to embrace, and with a strong sympathy to share, the evils of others, even with an unshrinking firmness superior to that of those whose misfortunes or vices induced them—are amongst the qualities which the actual treatment of women has developed in them ; and in which men are wretchedly deficient. In passive courage, in enduring, persevering, fortitude, women are undoubtedly superior to men. Even to death, the number of heroic submissions have been greater in proportion to the number sacrificed by the brutality of their fellow-creatures, amongst women than amongst men.

In the exercise of political functions, legislative, judicial, or others, is it active or passive courage that is wanting? is it patience and perseverance, or heedlessness of danger? is it the warrior's or the nurse's qualities? It is assuredly that species of activity which characterizes the nurse rather than that which characterizes the warrior: it is not the activity which will lift much, run much, or slay much, but which will watch much and with never-ceasing patience endure much. So far then, contrasting the two constitutional, or chiefly perhaps acquired, species of activity, of which women and men are actually possessed, without seeking for more from altered circumstances, the advantage would appear to be on the side of women. Women have the habit and the capacity for that species of activity which is most appropriate to the end in view. Certainly they would not be inclined or able to fight for their laws, as male legislators are so fond of doing, or hiring others to do ; but they would on that very account be the more inclined so to study and enact their laws, so to frame their judgements, that they would carry their own recommendation with them, that they would want no support from the sword or the bayonet, but would find their unbought support in the interests of the immense majority of those, with whose actions, or the fruits of whose labor, they interfered. What has every where made laws so vicious, even beyond the want of knowledge in the framers of them? The *force* which the law-makers have always had at hand to compel obedience: whence the superfluousness of wisdom or of consulting the interests of those on whom the laws were imposed. Active talent indeed, and in too great quantity, have male legislators possessed: just that species of activity however which was necessary to cause unjust and unequal laws to be obeyed, not that species of activity which would endure watchings and privations in order to make just laws. So beloved has been this instrument of force by these male sages, that we know it *used* to be made the judicial proof of what was right in private affairs—trial by battle—and *still is* the universal standard of rectitude in national affairs—decision by the brute force of war! Hard indeed for women to exercise political power so wisely as men have done!

Still nature has given man an advantage in point of active talent, enough to counterbalance perhaps the ill-direction of that particular species of this talent which he possesses. Though from his frequent abuse of strength, and ignorant self-will in exposing himself to intemperance and other causes injurious to health, he is more frequently incapacitated, from factitious causes of his own formation, from the regular exercise of his faculties than women are, yet is he not like woman liable to any natural cause of interruption to his pursuits. To this natural cause of distraction from duties ever so important, women are occasionally liable from the inconveniences of gestation; though not possibly to a greater extent, occupying more time on an average out of the twelve months, than men are liable to from the numerous permanent diseases, as well as occasional excesses brought on them by their imprudence, intemperance, and distractions of other vices. When a man's frame is deranged by a disease brought on by his own pernicious folly, and is thus incapacitated from attending to the most important affairs, he is pitied, and those are esteemed very unreasonable who do not accept of his illness as a sufficient excuse for the neglect of their business, though ever so important. But if a woman, without being even accused of any vice or folly, is incapacitated by pain, the necessary result of organization, and indispensable for the very existence of the human race, from attending for a time to duties equally important, she is *ridiculed,* and those are ridiculed who suffer their affairs to be liable to such interruption. Oh! heartless race of men! how long will ye taunt and revile the victims whom ye oppress? how long shall mockery gloss over your cruelty to others for occurrences which are virtues when compared with your own self-induced incapacities and pains? Go to: your wretched quackery of applying sympathy, and more than sympathy, unmerited, indulgence to your own vices and their consequences, while you substitute sarcasm for reason, instead of affording sympathy, to casualties in which you cannot become partakers, will avail you no more. These vile expedients, played off for so many thousand years, are fast wearing away: hypocrisy, your old ally, is falling into disrepute: justice, in contempt of your likings and love of domination, shall judge impartially between the amount of evil likely to be caused by the natural, innocent, and otherwise useful interruptions to active exertion to which women are liable, and the factitious, mostly vicious, and otherwise pernicious, interruptions to active exertions which men almost always bring on themselves. First, three out of four of the women deputed to legislative and other political offices, would be about the same age that men now are who fill them, that is to say, beyond the age of child-bearing. Next, the fourth part, who would from age be liable to such casualties, would always have it in their power, if any strong motive demanded it, to prevent their occurrence. So that in the end, even supposing that every woman of the fourth part so liable was thus temporarily incapacitated every two or three years, the amount of the evil would be, that one eighth or one twelfth of the whole number employed would every year be necessarily absent and incapable of performing their duties for one month or six weeks out of the year! Twelve persons may be absent for one month each, to be equal to the absence of one for the whole year. To ascertain then the quantity of permanent absence, we must divide the one eighth of the whole number by twelve; and should the whole number employed be four hundred, and the one eighth, or fifty, thereof be divided by twelve, we shall have four and a small fraction, or about one per cent for the permanently absent from this cause! How perfectly insignificant is the mischief, how much beneath all contempt is the ridicule sought to be thrown on the active exertions of intelligent women from this cause! Shameless slanderers! as ye are; heartless hypocrites! look to your legislative, your *representative*, assembly as ye term it, your six hundred and fifty-eight *men*, night after night dismissed because forty are not present, occupied in all the rounds of sensuality and other vices, enslaving and preying upon the very women whom ye slander; and then, if the net-work between the terminations of your arteries and veins has not become impervious to the indignant blood, blush, if ye can blush where women are concerned—blush for your impotent ridicule, for your affectation of mischief arising from such a cause to the active mental exertions of a number of women!

But it may be said that under a real representative system, and not a sham representation covering over the iniquities of an insolent oligarchy, this shameful neglect of duties in male representatives would not occur. True: let your male representatives be as actively and usefully employed as *want of power to do mischief* will compel them to be; let displacement be prompt and certain, not waiting to the end of seven or of three years, or of one year if they betray their trust; and you may then compare them in point of really appropriate active talent for political duties with women, over whom, as exclusive legislators, nature, or the organization of man in his possession of superior strength, has given him an ever-efficient check.

Women, however, are no more exempt from the casualties of disease and accident, not brought on by their own vice and folly, than men are; and if we suppose, from the temptation of superior strength affording ampler opportunities to men, that the disturbances arising from vice and folly are so much more frequent with them as to counterbalance the natural disturbance to the exercise of active talent in women, we shall have a scale of probabilities in which it will be hard to determine on which side the balance lies.

Thus does it appear that of the three qualities or species of talent—viz. moral aptitude or probity, intellectual aptitude or wisdom, and activity—requisite for the exclusive possessors of political power, women, as exclusively possessing those powers, would excel men as exclusive possessors of them in the first, or probity ; would be equal to them in the second, or appropriate wisdom ; and the degree in which, from a contest of probabilities, men would excel them in the latter, or appropriate activity—that activity which such peculiar duties demand—would be, if any thing, so small as not to be worthy of being taken into the account. We must then weigh the value of these two qualities, the first and the last, probity and activity; in the former of which women must under the supposed circumstances so much excel men, and in the latter of which men may so doubtfully excel women. Political probity, or a sympathy with the enjoyments and sincere desire to promote the happiness of all liable to be influenced by political measures, is a quality of such transcendent importance, that the other two together could by no means be put into comparison with it. Possessed of probity, every evil is shared, every means of happiness is turned to the best account. So ample are our susceptibilities to enjoyment from very slender means, provided we do not thwart, but benevolently promote each other's views, that this one quality of probity once established, human life would gradually transform itself into a paradise, and the alterations consequent on superior degrees of wisdom and activity would but give increased intensity and expansion to what was already delightful. But let wisdom or intellectual aptitude (in such a case, when divested of benevolence, more appropriately called cunning), along with ever so much of active talent, be given to those divested of the desire to make those qualities instrumental in promoting the happiness of their fellow-creatures, and it will be found that the more of these qualities is possessed by such beings, the more wretched will all liable to their operation become. In the one case, it will be a variety in point of intensity of happiness; in the other, a variety in point of intensity of vice, crime, and misery. Good intention, though ever so unintelligent, if without *the physical force requisite to make its follies operative,* as we are here supposing, could not do any permanent mischief; the moment it saw the evil operation of measures, it would change them: but to the evils likely to arise from extensive knowledge and skill combined with activity, and guided by selfishness, who shall set bounds? Men, as exclusive legislators, have always the physical power to trample on the happiness of the weaker half of the race: women are necessarily, and fortunately for such functions, divested of the power, and are therefore driven to political probity as a succedaneum for the want of force.

If therefore a community of rational beings, desirous of promoting equally the happiness of all—and without this desire they are divested of the noblest attribute of rationality—consisting, as the human race does, of an equal number of men and women, were driven to the absurd necessity of investing all political rights exclusively in the stronger or the weaker portion of the race, instead of investing the best and most intelligent with them, whether stronger or weaker, it would be evidently the interest of the whole to choose the weaker part, women, rather than the stronger part, men, for the exercise of such rights, both as electors and elected.

It is not forgotten that the condition of this second question, was the supposition that the interests of one half the race were absolutely involved in the other, thus taking for granted an equal degree of moral aptitude in the two divisions of the race, for the exercise of political rights. But if from the analysis we have gone through, there is a strong probability that the moral aptitude would be greater on the side of the weaker, it will show more strongly the odiousness of the injustice which, without inquiry, gives to the stronger as a matter of course those exclusive powers, which superior strength necessarily impels any thing short of comprehensive and benevolent wisdom to abuse.

In fact, suppose that the interests of women and men were ever so much involved, or that the interests of any portion of the adult part of men or women were ever so much involved in those of the remaining portion of women or men—what *harm* could it do, that the portion whose interests were so involved should themselves exercise equally with the rest of their fellow-creatures all political rights? To them it would be a pleasure, a most innocent, it has been shown a most useful and improving, species of pleasure. Why deprive them of it? Is it not a species of pleasure which costs nothing, which would procure additional respect and consideration for the holders of it? which would increase the general mass of intelligent communication, of sympathy and happiness? If interests be involved, what benefit can be derived to any one from excluding any one sane adult human being? Whom can such exclusion serve? to whom can it give any pleasure—the pleasure of using it as an engine of ulterior oppression being for the present supposed not to exist? It could give no pleasure, but a vicious pleasure (or one attended with preponderant mischief) to any minds. To such only as could find pleasure in the contemplation of the inferiority, that is to say, of the comparative misery, of their fellow-creatures, could the exclusion be pleasing. The happiness lost to the individuals tormented by such a state of mind as love of superiority without merit is beyond calculation. The happiness of the persons indulging an opposite feeling is liable to be increased by the pleasures in proportion to their intensity, whether less or more than theirs, of all around them. The immense accession of happiness, from reflected pleasures, from sympathy, is hardly to be described; more than a thousand fold it increases happiness. Even in the absence of personal happiness, even under the pressure of positive pain, it can supply at intervals the wonted glow of enjoyment. Nothing but positive personal want, or the malevolence of others directly operating upon them, can prevent the wise from eagerly seizing and making the most of all those abundantly existing sources of joy from sympathy with the pleasures of others. How baneful then even to the usurping excluders is the exercise of so malevolent a power over the equal love of happiness, and the free exercise of all their powers as one of the chief constituents of that happiness, of their fellow-creatures! In *justice to the stronger excluding party*, all such power of exclusion should be withheld. Most certain it unfortunately is, that under the present system of labor and exertion by individual competition, the interests of all, first for existence and then for splendor, are put in such rude opposition to each other, that they render almost impossible the developement to any great extent of these kindly feelings of joy in the welfare of others. Till other arrangements of "mutual co-operation" are formed, by means of which personal interests, either for the supply of immediate wants or of all desirable conveniences, instead of being opposed to feelings of benevolence as they now are, shall move uniformly in the same direction with them, all, or almost all the cheap and delightful pleasures of sympathy and benevolence must be lost to mankind: so difficult is it for the bulk of men to extend their views, in opposition to immediate interest, into the distant consequences of actions in the doubtful future. While sympathy urges us to rejoice in the expressive smiles of another's happiness, the habitual distrust of competition tells us such happiness was procured at our expense, or that it upbraids our unsuccessful efforts, or is treading on the heels of our superior success. All the blessings of life are turned into curses. Yes, it is only under the system of voluntary associated labor and exertion and equal distribution, that justice can have free scope, that the equal rights of all can prevail, and that women can become in intelligence, virtue and happiness, the equals of regenerated men. how much unlike, how much superior to, the bullying, suspicious, and mere sensual creatures that are now called men!

Enough has perhaps been said to prove that the hypothesis, untenable as it has been shown to be, of an involving of interests does not justify, even if true, the exclusion of either party, particularly the weaker, from the possession of political rights; because one of the two leading benefits of political rights, the improvement of the character and enlargement of the mind of the excluded, would be thereby prevented; because the weaker party would be more apt from necessity to make good laws for the benefit of the whole, than the stronger party; because both having equal claims, it would be impossible to satisfy the excluded party of the propriety of the exclusion, thus nurturing a constant stock of discontent; and because no possible injury, but, if rightly constituted, a pleasure of sympathy would arise to the excluding party, by the contemplation of the innocent and useful enjoyments conferred on the excluded party by the exercise of such rights. The general principle of mutual respect and benevolence would be immensely strengthened and diffused by the removal of exclusions.

Though nothing short of "voluntary association," or the " mutual co-operation of industry and talents in large numbers," would entirely heal the flagrant evils of our present artificial social system, and particularly the desolating injustice practised on women; yet would the mere removal of restraints, of exclusions and unequal laws, so improve their situation and the general aspect of human intercourse, that they would be no longer recognised for the same. There are two great advances in the progress of human improvement, the one positive, the other negative: the negative consisting in the removal of restraints; the positive in the voluntary establishment of co-operative associations. These two advances are not incompatible with each other; but the one, the removal of restraints, leading to the other, and to a certain extent necessary to its establishment. The removal of the barbarous restraints that now every where tie up the industry and talents, that freeze the intellect and sympathies of men, would put them into a situation to examine their organization and capacities of enjoyment, and the physical and moral means of gratifying them. Then, if found useful by free and rational beings seeking their happiness, would be every where adopted the magnificent system of "voluntary association," by equal contributions of all the various faculties of all, mental or bodily, for the equal enjoyment of all; as a basis on which to found the future physical, intellectual, and moral improvement of the human race.

PART II.

Question III.—*Is there in the nature of things, any security for equality of enjoyments, proportioned to exertion and capabilities, but by means of equal civil rights ? or any security for equal civil, but by means of equal political, rights ?*

TOPICS OF QUESTION III.

First.—" Can women enjoy equal chances of happiness with men without equal *civil* and *criminal* laws ?" 155

The organization of man gives him great advantages in the pursuit of happiness over women : therefore, ... 155

Even under a system of perfectly free and equal competition, as resulting from equal civil rights, restraints, and punishments, there would still remain *natural* bars to the acquisition by women of equal happiness with men 156

All that is asked for on the part of women is, that to these natural bars no *artificial* restraints should be superadded; no unequal laws, civil or criminal 158

Hence a physical reason, peculiar to women, rendering *more* necessary to them than to men equal civil and criminal laws; the greatest equality of civil rights being less available in their hands, than in those of men, to the attainment of equal happiness . 158

Claims or demands of women stated 159

The combined force of law and public opinion is equally unjust to women. Public opinion, if even in their favor, would not, in the absence of equal laws, be a sufficient guarantee for equal chances of enjoyment. Public opinion would little influence the ignorant and brutal, whom it is most necessary to restrain 160

Though public opinion might remove the evils of voluntary oppression, it could not abate the evils of partial legal exclusions, the enforcements of which do not depend on individual volition. Nothing but the *repeal* of such unequal laws can abate their mischief . 162

Unequal laws degrade women in their own eyes; then in those of men 164

Qu. 3.] *Topics of Question the Third.* 153

Second.—"Can women possess any guarantee for the establishment and continuance of equal civil and criminal laws, but by means of the possession of equal *political* laws?" 166
If the desire be sincere of affording equal chances of enjoyment by equal exertions to women and men, of removing all unequal penalties and restraints, no just motive can remain for excluding women from political rights, the plain and obvious guarantee of these advantages 168
Suppose that civil and criminal laws were equal, that sexual morals were forgotten; what right have men to monopolize from women the *pleasure of electing and being elected?* what right have they to deprive women of the *other advantages* shown to arise from the exercise of political rights? 168
The history of the human race affords no example of the conceding of equal civil rights and chances of enjoyment to those excluded from political rights 170
Without equal political rights, equal civil and criminal laws could not be *executed* 172
Without equal political laws, one third *plus one* of the whole adults of the human race, would control three fourths *less one*. 174
Without equal political rights, legislators cannot *know* the wishes of women as to their interests 174
Physical circumstances necessitating greater attention of women to narrow views of domestic concerns, these require to be counteracted, *more* than in men, by political rights, the exercise of which leads to comprehensive views of extended benevolence . . . 177
Natural tendencies, whether physical or moral, should be nursed and encouraged when useful; when attended with preponderant mischief, should be counteracted or modified 181
Summary argument for political rights 182
The real danger is, that even these constitutional guarantees to women would be inefficient to their protection 183
General question of the state of women is irrelevant to present discussion 186

ADDRESS TO WOMEN.

Inherent love of happiness is the basis on which reason must ultimately operate to open the eyes of women 188

All useful qualities, all qualities tending to the happiness of women as rational independent beings, are now, by the systematic jealousy of men, repressed in women. Man suffers no qualities to be cultivated in woman but such as are subservient to his own immediate enjoyment 189

Under all past arrangements of society, despotic or republican, women have been every where, and nearly alike, the slaves of men 196

Under no system of social arrangements founded on individual competition for individual wealth can women enjoy equal happiness with men 198

A social system, founded on the mutual co-operation of large numbers of men and women, can alone ensure it to them . . . 199

While community of property would deprive men of the means of oppression, it would remove all motives from women to submission to any species of factitious inequality 200

Men, receiving the intellectual and moral benefits of equality from women, become their equals, would be indebted to them for the greatest boon ever conferred on the human race . . . 208

PART II.

QUESTION III.—*Is there in the nature of things, any security for equality of enjoyments, proportioned to exertion and capabilities, but by means of equal civil rights? or any security for equal civil, but by means of equal political, rights?*

DISMISSING all pretensions on the part of men to the desire of doing equal justice to women, as falsified by the mere fact of withholding from them equal rights or legal protection, can we find out, first, any other guarantee for an equality between women and men, of enjoyments, proportioned to natural or acquired talents, than an equality of civil rights and criminal responsibilities? and next, can we find any other guarantee for the establishment or continuance of equal civil and criminal laws, as affecting men and women, than a perfect equality of political rights?

I. As the first in order, let us inquire whether any other guarantee can be given to women for equal chances of enjoyment with men, than an equality of *civil* and *criminal* laws.

The organization of man has given him, as an animal, tremendous advantages over woman in all his commerce with her, as well as in the pursuit and acquisition of all objects of desire, the supposed means of happiness. These advantages are superior muscular strength and the continued attention which he is able to devote to the object before him, uninterrupted by the pains and disabilities of gestation. In the earlier stages of society, when man had to contend with other animals and with other men of his own race for the means of existence, particularly food; and in subsequent periods, when the earth was to be cleared of timber and other obstacles in order to be cultivated for food, and when wars of antipathy succeeded to wars for subsistence—muscular strength and activity were the qualities most useful, not only for the comfort but for the very existence of the race. Of knowledge there was little, and that so easily acquired by the education of circumstances and engaging in the ordinary operations of the tribe or community, that no great source of distinction could arise from the possession of greater or smaller portions of it. The advantages of strength were little shared with any other quality; they were super-eminent. In all rude stages of society, women, even under the most free system of individual competition, must enjoy less than men, because their physical powers of acquiring are less than those of men.

It may well be asked, " Under such circumstances, where the field of competition for all articles of enjoyment, to be obtained chiefly through labor or the exertion of strength, is equally open to both parties, to women as to men, how can it be expected that women, being, on an average and with equal culture, deficient in strength and aptitude for uninterrupted effort, could attain to equal enjoyments, supposing even equal quantities of skill and knowledge with men to be in their possession?" Undoubtedly, this natural bar, under the system of labor or industry by individual competition, not admitting of compensations, is sufficient to keep down the average enjoyments of women beneath those of men.

Now in asking for equal domestic and other civil rights

Qu. 3.] *Disadvantages would remain against Women.* 157

with men, women do not ask for the removal of any of these natural bars to equality of enjoyment. They ask even for no compensations for these natural evils, such compensations being irreconcileable with the present scheme of society—that of labor or exertion by individual competition—and only to be afforded them by the system of mutual co-operation of large numbers.

If then this inequality of enjoyments from inequality of some of the human faculties be an unavoidable evil, what do women want? what do they mean by exclaiming against it? Man has not given himself this superiority of physical organization : he finds himself possessed of it; it is inalienable; it cannot be transferred or shared. Should force intervene to equalize enjoyments, and to give to the weak the produce of the labor of the strong? If to give it to women, why not to weak men? If every person be not secured in the products of his labor and the free disposal of those products, what will become of production? Who will be industrious, if what he earns by labor or voluntary exchange is arbitrarily taken from him and given to another, man or woman, without his consent? What would become of the industry of women themselves, under individual competition, if they were led to depend on the seizure of the fruits of the industry of men for the gratification of their wants?

Where the system of individual competition at all exists, all the evils here stated, with numberless other evils not named, as arising from interference with the *perfect freedom* of that competition according to the qualities, natural or acquired, of mind or body, of the industrious competitors, are allowed in their fullest extent. Women do not require any such interference in their favor. They require no more of enjoyment than what their faculties, whatever they may turn out to be, equally cultivated with those of men, may be able to procure for them under *equal* competition; competition free to all, and equal as to women with men. They expect no removal of natural bars to their success. All they ask is, that to these natural bars in the way of their pursuit of equal happiness with men, no additional bars, no *factitious restraints*, shall be superadded.

Is this an unreasonable request? Ought not men to remain satisfied, in the common pursuit of enjoyments or happiness, with those natural advantages of superior strength, uninterrupted exertion, and, as they themselves allege, of superior mental capability, which their organization has given them? With such superior faculties on the part of men, all other things being left equal between them and women, can there be a doubt as to which of the two the greater quantity of enjoyments must fall, from the greater facility in acquiring the means of enjoyment? If men afford nothing by way of compensation to women for these natural sources of inequality in acquisition and enjoyment, ought they to do any thing in the way of aggravation? Ought not women to be permitted the full and unmolested enjoyment of whatever these limited faculties, fully developed, and in the field of free competition, can procure for them, just as to men is secured the free enjoyment of what the free use of their improved faculties can procure for them? If you leave to man his superior acquisitions derived from superior powers, why not leave to woman her inferior acquisitions derived from inferior powers?

Now this is all that is meant by affording to women (under the system of individual competition) equal enjoyments with men. The simple and modest request is, that they may be permitted equal enjoyments with men, *provided they can by the free and equal developement and exercise of their faculties procure for themselves such enjoyments.* They ask the same means that men possess of acquiring every species of knowledge, of unfolding every one of their faculties of mind and body that can be made tributary to their happiness. They ask every facility of access to every art, occupation, profession, from the highest to the lowest, without one exception, to which their inclination and talents may direct and may fit them to occupy. They ask the removal of *all* restraints anc exclusions not applicable to men of equal capacities. They ask for perfectly equal political, civil and domestic rights. They ask for equal obligations and equal punishments from the law with men in case of infraction of the same law by either party. They ask for an equal system of morals, founded on utility instead of caprice and unreasoning despotism, in which the same action attended with the same consequences, whether done by man or woman, should be attended with the same portion of approbation or disapprobation; in which every pleasure, accompanied or followed by no preponderant evil, should be equally permitted to women and to men; in which every pleasure accompanied or followed by preponderant evil should be equally censured in women and in men.

Now how is it possible that this equality of enjoyments, proportioned to natural or acquired powers, should ever be attained by women, if they are by laws, regulations, or the diseased arbitrary will of men called public opinion, debarred from the equal culture of their natural powers or faculties with men ? or if they are excluded from the equal exercise of those improved faculties in whatever mode of action they may to them be usefully employed? or if the criminal laws, or what are miscalled morals, inflict on women more severe punishments or inconveniences, for the same real or imaginary offences, than they inflict on men? How is it possible to conceive, that women could have equal enjoyments with men, without equal civil and criminal laws, and a just or equal system of morals? It is plainly impossible. To tell women they may enjoy equally with men, while by civil and criminal laws you withhold from them the means of enjoyment, and by malicious antipathy, under the name of morals, torment them if they dare so to enjoy—is unworthy mockery.

Civil and criminal laws are formed by the state of public opinion, at least amongst the law-makers, whatever that may be, depending on the quantum of knowledge possessed. These laws, once established, powerfully re-act on public opinion. When in accordance with each other, these two, laws and public opinion, form a force, partly moral partly physical, which, when ill-directed, produce as much human misery, as when well-directed they produce good. In the case of women, they are both of them unequal, unjust and cruel, productive of vice and misery incalculable to both men and women. Now suppose that one of these powers began to be relaxed in its self-consuming malignity; suppose, as naturally occurs, that public opinion first begins to relent, to re-consider its judgements, and to suspect that in tormenting others it has wantonly deprived them of great sources of happiness, and has at the same time dashed from its own lips a thousand sources of intellectual and moral sympathy—and all for the brute gratification of the pleasure of unreasoning command! Suppose this:

could this change in public opinion, as to the mischievousness of unequal laws, involving unequal rights and unequal punishments, of unequal means of developing natural powers, of unequal opportunities for the exercise of those powers, produce equality of enjoyments? Could it, without a corresponding change in the laws, render equal justice to women?

On this head there are a great many distinctions to be made. All the well-disposed part of the public yielding to, or participating in, the force of this improved public opinion, would act towards women, as far as lay in their power, as if no such exclusive or partial laws existed. As far as it depended on them to aid in the execution of any such exclusive laws, they might withdraw their co-operation. Just fathers might leave their property equally between their children, sons and daughters, and might *endeavour* to give an equally enlarged education to each. Just husbands might yield the same power of judging and acting to their wives, the same freedom in every respect, the same command over their own property (the fortune they possessed at marriage), and the annual consumable revenue, from whatever source derived, that they themselves enjoyed: they might disdain to avail themselves of the fiend-like malignity of partial laws; they might reject any further bond on their wives' affections than that which their wives have on theirs, namely, the power, by kindness, justice and reason, of pleasing. The public in general might judge of the actions of women, as to morality or immorality, by the same standard by which they judged of the actions of men. But this conduct of the well-disposed amongst men, say in this supposed improved state of things of the great majority of men, would not take away an atom from the ill-disposed, the small minority of men, of the legal power, very little from the inclination, of practising their old domestic atrocities of despotism, and of availing themselves of the still existing laws whenever they enabled them to crush their victims. Not only would all the unjust be uncurbed—on whose pernicious passions and ignorance a restraint is the most necessary—but no security could women have for the continuance of the good conduct of any of the seemingly good. How few continue consistently good all their lives! How hard is it for the holder of despotic power to judge impartially in his own case! With what bitterness of apprehension must all these permissions of equality, these licences to be happy, be received by women! Permissions from equals, where no power of permission ought to exist! permissions to be moral and beneficent, and to reap the fruits of beneficence and morality! The elevated soul sickens at such permissions; the mind of an elevated man would sicken at the humiliation of having to grant to a friend and an equal such permissions.

But this is not all. It is but a very small part of the exclusions or unequal laws affecting women, which depend on the co-operation of men, well- or ill-disposed, for their execution. In all these cases public opinion, even the most enlightened, would be of no use to women without the repeal of such exclusive or partial laws. Such are the laws affecting intestate property, particularly of land, preferring male heirs; such are the laws excluding women, directly or indirectly, from almost all lucrative, professional or intellectual, occupations; excluding them from places of education in all the higher branches of knowledge; excluding them, when married, from protection from personal assaults and restraints; excluding them from the same means of getting rid of a worthless and vicious husband, that men have to free themselves from wives ever so affectionate and exalted, should they once retaliate one of the thousand infidelities of their husbands. As long as these positive exclusions and monopolies of barbaric ignorance and jealousy remain, so long will enlightened public opinion and private beneficence be impotent in endeavouring to raise women in the eyes of men to that respect which equals alone can claim and receive from equals. How should women acquire equal knowledge with men, if equal means of instruction, similar to those afforded to men at colleges and elsewhere, are not to them equally afforded? Or, if such means were afforded, what motives would remain to women to avail themselves of such advantages, as long as all those arts, professions, pursuits, and offices are withheld from them, though ever so deserving, to prepare for the proper discharge of which such knowledge, physical or moral, is chiefly sought for at such establishments by men? If they got the knowledge, how could they make it available, under the system of competition, to the increase of their enjoyments, if they could not, like men, turn it, through trades or professsions, to a pecuniary account, to procure the means of enjoyment, and of pecuniary independence, as one of the most essential of those means in the present state of social intercourse? It is altogether childish, therefore, to talk of an improved public opinion, and the acquired beneficence of men, as capable of serving as a substitute to women for equal civil and criminal laws. No wishes, no kindly intentions, can conjure away exclusions, can alter laws. The laws must be repealed. If this public opinion be sincere, they will, as a matter of course, be repealed.

Though, from the indirect operation of numerous causes, few women might avail themselves of the removal of all existing exclusions and restraints; though the habits of men, in the possession of all arts, trades, professions, and employments, might long render them unwilling to elect women, though of superior merit, to places which men had been accustomed to occupy ; yet would the very eligibility be an incentive to knowledge and exertion amongst women: it would raise them in their own opinion : the barrier of sexual superiority and domination would be broken down : women would see a possibility, by means of improvement, of becoming the equals, not only in domestic but in civil life, with men. As they respected themselves and became respectable, the respect of men would follow on their own. Instead of being looked upon as the ignorant slaves of man's animal propensities, they would be the cultivated and equal sharers of the most exquisite mingled pleasures of sense and intellect of which human nature is susceptible. On the contrary, while these exclusions and unequal restraints remain on women, the brand of inferiority, of degradation is impressed upon them. To be a woman is to be an inferior animal; an inferiority by no talents, by no virtues, to be surmounted ; indelible like the skin of the Black ; man vainly seeking to throw on what he calls nature, or organization, the odium of this brand, the mere creature of his own ignorant selfishness and injustice. Thus branded with mental incapacity, with incapacity for every situation requiring comprehensiveness of view or enlargement of knowledge, how can man respect woman as his equal? how can he sympathize with her pleasures and pains as with those of an equal ? and if not, how can he render her equal justice ? how can he look upon her in any

Qu. 3.] *Equal Laws insecure without political Rights.* 165

other light than as belonging to an inferior class of beings, unentitled to equal consideration, equal happiness, with himself? Though the removal of the legal restraint or exclusion were never by woman taken advantage of, yet while it exists she must ever remain, as she now is, a degraded being, compared with them in whose favour the restraint or exclusion against her is upheld—degraded in her own eyes, and in theirs degraded.

Now this feeling of superiority on one side, and of inferiority on the other, necessarily followed as it is by antipathies, and those antipathies as necessarily followed by ill offices, many of them, though minute in description, overwhelmingly painful to the wounded mind, constitutes itself one of the greatest sources of unhappiness to which human beings are liable : it is enough to poison every cup of joy. To the really exalted and benevolent mind the one feeling, that of unmerited assumption of superiority, would be as odious as the other, that of submission to unmerited inferiority.

So far then it is evident that no change of public opinion, no kind treatment by men could procure for women an equal chance of enjoyment with men, without equal civil and criminal laws. We have now to ascend a step higher, and to suppose, that the improved public opinion and enlightened regard of men for their own happiness, and their tardy acknowledgement that the happiness of women ought to be as much promoted for their own sake as that of men for theirs, had removed all civil and criminal disqualifications and inequalities from women ; and that men reserved nothing more for themselves than the exclusive possession of *political* rights, the faculty, suppose, of electing and being elected to all legislative and administrative offices. Ought women, under an equal system of morals, founded on utility alone, or the tendency of actions to promote preponderant good, with a system of equal civil and criminal law, to rest satisfied? The answer is: if the exclusion from political rights tended to increase their happiness, or to render it more secure, they ought to remain satisfied without such rights; if, on the contrary, the exclusion from political rights tended to decrease their happiness, or to render the continuance of it less secure, they ought not to remain satisfied without such rights.

II. Our second proposition, That the happiness of women—and incalculably that of the whole race, as may be hereafter and elsewhere shown—would be much increased, though already enjoying an equal system of morals and laws, by an equality also of political rights, may appear from the following considerations.

Whatever may be said as to the possibility of being supremely happy by the permission of masters, no person will deny but that the more supremely happy this state is, the more certain it would be—that to be assured of the continuance, without almost the possibility of losing such supreme bliss, would be of itself an accession, and no inconsiderable accession, of delight to this blissful state. If we were but sure that our good masters would never change their minds, no other wish would remain for us: we might then give way to all the security of joy! How natural, how unavoidable, how wise, under such circumstances, such a sentiment! To this, to be sure, the more long-sighted would add: Aye, and if they could live for ever, we should then be secure indeed; but their descendants—who shall answer for them? is justice to be henceforth hereditary? may not future women fear that they may not be as fortunate as we in living under so upright a race of men?

There are those men, who, abashed at the iniquities of what is ludicrously styled the *marriage contract,* and at all the civil and moral exclusions to which women are subjected, when such matters are fairly put before them; who, wishing to see such fruitful sources of human vice and misery removed, still startle at the only measures which can be attended with even a chance of removing them under the present social system of individual competition for wealth. " True," they say, "the inequalities of mar-
" riage laws, the despotism of the stronger party, are no-
" thing but the odious remains of ancient barbarism, the
" abuse of the superior strength of the savage. Personal
" protection of law, redress and punishment for offences
" against each other in the marriage state, as in every other,
" ought to be equal: women ought to have as ample means
" of acquiring all species of knowledge and industrious oc-
" cupations as men: the disgrace ought to be abolished of
" sexual legislation and sexual morality awarding pernici-
" ous gratifications and impunity to men, to women endless
" privations, or destitution and death if they but touch a rose
" out of the heap with which man regales his bloated appe-
" tites. True, all the injustice ought to be rectified. Of two
" persons engaging in the same act, one ought not to be more
" severely punished than another. But why talk of *poli-*
" *tical* rights for women? Cannot all the barbarian laws,
" imposing these unequal restraints and punishments on
" the weaker instead of the stronger party, on whom, if on
" either, they ought to be imposed, be repealed, as they
" were made, by *men?* If women get equal means of edu-
" cation, equal civil and domestic rights, equal duties and

" no more than equal punishments for the infraction of
" these duties, with men, what more would they want?
" Of what further use would political rights be to them,
" than to obtain these advantages?"

A sufficient answer to all these repentant professions would perhaps be this. " If men be sincere in the desire of affording equal enjoyments to women, in proportion to their capacity, by means of faculties equally cultivated, and other means equally ample, of procuring for themselves such enjoyments; if they be sincere in the desire of yielding to women equal civil rights, as a means of procuring this equality of enjoyment—what motive could induce men so disposed still to withhold from women those political rights, which are the obvious means of procuring and preserving for them the protection of equal civil and criminal laws, the guarantee of equal chances of enjoyment? There must be some motive for this withholding, some lurking love of despotism." If the motive of the continuance of the political exclusions be not to oppress, is it to remind the enfranchised slaves that the *power* to oppress still continues? that the same hands which relaxed the chains can again impose them with double rivets? with the view of clinging to the ghost of despotism, when its substance is surrendered? with the view of dropping deadly poison, the poison of apprehension, of insecurity, into the cup of equal justice, which reason has from unwilling hands extorted? Or if these be not the motives, are they to be found in the desire of men of retaining in their own hands the pleasure of the exercise, say of the benevolent exercise, of political powers? a species of pleasure, that of electing or being elected, which it is no more just they should exclude women from an equal chance of obtaining by superior merit, at the free choice of their fellow-creatures, than any other species of pleasure whatever. Nothing is more evident than that there must be some motive of apparent advantage to those who exclude others, though not showing itself in the shape of unequal regulations: and it is equally evident that that apparent advantage cannot be obtained but at the expense of the excluded.

Again—the assumption involved in these repentant professions is not true. It is not true that all the good that can be derived to women from the possession of equal political rights with men, is the equality of civil and criminal laws between them and men. It has been shown that a second advantage, the expansion of the mind, of the intellectual powers, and of the sympathies of benevolence, depends on the exercise of these powers; and that without this comprehensiveness of mind and benevolence, some of the greatest enjoyments arising from civil equality would be lost as they would all be lessened. The desire, therefore, ever so great and so sincere on the part of men, of using their exclusive political power so as to restore to women an equal chance of enjoyment with themselves, by means of equal civil and criminal laws, would do absolutely nothing towards putting women in possession of this secondary train of advantages. The exercise of political rights does confer a great deal more of the means of happiness than the mere establishment of equal civil and criminal laws: particularly an equal system of private morals, and of the sanctions of public opinion, can never be brought into being but as the result of that comprehensiveness of mind and sympathy which political rights are the most efficient means of unfolding.

But of what avail these pretensions of the wish to do

justice when coupled with the obstinate retaining of the power to do injustice? the exclusive power of making at pleasure unequal laws, with the sincere wish of making none but those that are equal? What does, in fact, the author of the "Article on Government" think of such speechifying pretences when set forth by men excluding other men, similarly organized with themselves, with whose pleasures and pains they are more likely to sympathize than with those of women, and whose equal strength might serve as a check on their selfish propensities? He looks, and he justly looks, on all such pretences, under such circumstances, of the wish to do good, as audacious hypocrisy; and he refers to the uniform *undeviating conduct* of all men and of all bodies or clubs of men possessing exclusive power, as demonstration of this hypocrisy. Now if privileges, direct or indirect, in favor of the possessors of power, and privations and indignities towards the non-possessors, have been uniformly the effect of exclusions from political rights; and if these unerring consequences be demonstration of the hollowness of the pretext of the desire to use exclusive power for the equal happiness of the excluded and the excluders, when men are the party excluded by men; how infinitely more flagrant must the hypocrisy appear when made use of by men possessing exclusive power towards women? If the conduct of men possessing exclusive political powers has been unjust to their fellow-men, has it not been atrocious every where, even in what are called the most civilized countries, towards women? Every where but in the most barbarous countries the increasing knowledge of exclusive legislators has abolished personal slavery—the substitution of individual caprice for an appeal to the laws—in respect to men. Every where, even with respect to the most exalted of women, in talents and virtues most exalted, have exclusive male legislators retained and enforced, and still uphold, the horrid system of domestic slavery, slavery of the most glorious of women, in marriage, to the most vile of men, for the crime (the law has erected the physical organization into a crime) of being a woman! Affect wonder at the hypocrisy of men when so acting and so pretending to their own sex, and put forth yourself pretensions and hypocrisy a thousand times more glaring when the weaker half of the human race is concerned! Alas! inconsistent man, and inconsistent philosophy; wherefore is your boasted pole-star of the principle of utility so soon eclipsed? If the absolute conduct of men, the possessors of, towards those excluded from, political rights, is demonstration of the falsehood of pretended good intentions, how much more strong must the demonstration be towards women, where the conduct has been so immeasurably more at variance with professions! But the principle of utility has been hitherto applied by the greater part even of the most liberal of those using it, as if it meant the tendency of things to promote the greatest happiness, not of the human race in general, of the whole race, but of *one moiety of the race*, men. As inquisitors, or as men possessing political power, are in the habit of applying the word Utility to all those things which tend to promote their own individual happiness under the cabalistic terms Church and State, so have pretended philosophers, somewhat less vicious and absurd, applied it to those things which tend to promote the exclusive happiness of the sex to which they belong; inquisitors, politicians, and philosophers, equally satisfied in their bloated selfishness, vanity, and presumption, that provided their own well-being is taken care of, that of all other human beings must necessarily be included or *involved* in it. Most short and convenient recipe for satisfying the demands of equal justice! It is only to assume unlimited benevolence and unerring knowledge and wisdom on the part of the possessors of power, and the thing is done entirely to the satisfaction of those who exclude their fellow-creatures!

Political rights are necessary to women as a check on the almost inveterate habits of exclusion of men. It is in vain to sanction by law a civil right, or to remove an exclusion, if the law affords no means to those whom it designs to benefit of causing the right or permission to be enforced. Women may be eligible by law to the situation of professors; the law may protect them when married from the personal violence or constraint of any kind of their husbands, as fully as it protects husbands against them ; but if none but men are to be the electors, if none but men are to be jurors or judges when women complain against men of partiality and injustice, is it in human nature that a sympathy from old habit, from similarity of organization and trains of thought, from love of domination, should not have a tendency to make men swerve from the line of justice and strict impartiality, should not make them underrate the pretensions of women, and be lenient to the errors of men? When to this are joined the superior strength, the *secrecy* of domestic wrongs, and thence the means of transgression and impunity, who can doubt the necessity of an equally mixed, as resulting from equal political laws, in order to be an impartial, tribunal, in all cases where women are the parties as against men, or men as against women? True that under the shield of equal laws and equal morals, such cases would bear but a small proportion to the whole number of cases brought into judgement, the greater proportion of them being unconnected with sexual concerns; in all which cases men or women, as found most convenient, would naturally discharge the duties: but why, in cases where men are necessarily interested parties, give them a monopoly of judging? Though the present exclusions of women, particularly in marriage, from most of the rights of property, as well as from almost all other rights, were removed, it is very probable that, partly from want of inclination, partly from motives of convenience, numbers of women qualified would not offer themselves for offices, and would not exercise their political rights; yet would the consciousness in the minds of men of such powers of control existing amongst women cause them so to regulate their conduct, as to render for the most part unnecessary any party display of their power. In all cases where partiality was only suspected, women would of course exercise their rights. If but few women were themselves elected as representatives, their influence would cause such men to be elected as would enact equal laws between the two great portions of the race, or would cause such men as showed an inclination to revive the old reign of brutality and injustice to be replaced by other men or by women. Now is it possible to conceive that any set of legislators, male or female, particularly men, would not be more inclined to make and preserve laws of entire reciprocity and equal justice between women and men, when they knew that their constituents were equally balanced, and that injustice on their part would necessarily enlist a few of either party amongst the injured half, and thus create a majority of the whole constituents against them? Under the system of exclusive political rights, though nearly one half of men joined with the whole of women in reprobation of unequal laws, those laws, as long as there was a majority of one of the whole males in favor of injustice, could persevere in injustice, in contempt of the wishes of three fourths, wanting one, of the whole race. Under the system of non-exclusion, *all men* but one could not effect injustice against women. The one just man giving his casting vote to the equal votes of women, would wipe away from men the opprobrium of the meditated wrong. Who can doubt then of the necessity of the enjoyment of equal political rights by women as a preservative against the possibility of the monstrous evil of three fourths, *wanting one,* of every community being every day liable to be oppressed by one fourth, *plus one?* Nothing less than giving equal rights to all, men and women, can guard against such evils, can promote the equal happiness of all.

A second reason why women, in addition to equal laws and an equal system of morals, should also possess equal political rights and be eligible to all offices, (if so disposed, and not by rotation or compulsion,) like men, is, that exclusive legislators, particularly men as exclusive legislators for women, though ever so sincerely inclined to promote the happiness of those whom they exclude equally with their own, must be liable to errors from want of knowledge, from *false judgements*. How can exclusive legislators know the interests of those who are not their constituents, of those whom they never consult, who have no control over them? not what they, the legislators, are pleased arbitrarily to call their interests without having any intercourse with them, without any means of discovering them, but what the excluded themselves think to be their interest? or at least what those amongst the excluded who choose to think at all, deem to be their interest? In case of difference of opinion between legislators and those for whose benefit regulations are said to be made, (as suppose the insolent and stultifying law or custom of preventing women from addressing numbers of their fellow-creatures in a public room or assembly,) how is the legislator to find out this opinion, when none of those affected by the regulation, and who choose to think at all about it, have any means of making their sentiments known to him as their representative? In all cases of difference of opinion between legislators and constituents, it is the duty of legislators to enlighten and convince their constituents before they presume to dragoon them into pretended interests which they disclaim. But how can legislators enlighten constituents whom they do not know? how can legislators know when those constituents are convinced, if they have no mode by their votes of expressing their opinions? if all those whose opinions are permitted by their votes to be expressed are necessarily either indifferent or hostile to those whose interests are in question? as is the case with respect to men where the interests of women alone are concerned. What is one of the eternal excuses for iniquitous legislation, on the part of those who affect to take into consideration the influence of their measures not only on their own interests but on those also of all others liable to be affected by them? Is it not the pretence that the measures in question do really promote the interests of those whom they affect? What means so simple and effectual, what other practicable means are there, of silencing for ever this pretext, or gratifying the allegation if sincere, as affording the means of collecting by personal vote the opinions of those whose interests are at stake? Till this simple expedient is resorted to, any interests, at the will of the law-makers, may be said to be promoted by any measures. But let those affected by the measure stand in the relation of constituents to its enactors, and let it be imperative under pain of recal, on those enactors, to suspend legislating until they have convinced those of their constituents, or the majority of them, who choose to think at all upon the subject, that the proposed measures really promote their interest, and all difficulties as to errors of judgement in legislators will be removed. Women will no longer be insulted with barbarous laws, and then coolly told by the enactors of them that they are really for their interest, inasmuch as their interests are, by a wise and mysterious dispensation of nature, involved always in the interests of the exclusive male lawmakers, or their exclusive male constituents. The laws affecting the interest of women alone, which in the opinion of the enlightened and influential amongst women tended to their happiness, would be the only ones enacted, had women equal political rights with men. Those affecting the interests of both men and women would be enacted when desired or assented to by the majority of both. The evil of making laws for the pretended benefit, but in contempt of the will, of human beings, being absolutely without measure, while the evil of waiting for the approbation, or at least assent, of the majority of those interested and inclined to judge, being as nothing, but attended with effects in almost every way salutary; it is clear that the latter is the only method of reducing to the lowest the mischiefs of false judgement on the part of

Qu. 3.] *Domesticity requires Check of Political Rights.*

well-disposed legislators : and this scheme of persuasion cannot be carried into effect with respect to women but by investing them with equal political rights.

To these moral circumstances a physical circumstance is to be added, which of itself alone would demonstrate the most unqualified and indispensable necessity of political rights to women, in order to guaranty to them all the happiness which equal civil and criminal laws are calculated to afford. From the physical organization of women, as regards the bearing and rearing of children, (suppose that even the rearing terminated with weaning or at a year old,) they must, on an average, be more engaged in and more inclined to affairs of domesticity than men. Men, on an average, must, of the two, be more out of doors, more frequently mingling and associating with their fellow-creatures, more engaged in and conversant with the incidents and interests of large masses, of their country, or of society in general. Men must always have therefore superior opportunities of influence, of attaining their ends, of protecting themselves by indirect means without the protection which the direct check of political rights gives them. Even with respect to men, with all their advantages, it is every where found that where political rights are wanting, equal civil and criminal laws as between man and man are wanting also, and no more than partial snatches of happiness, or rather shadowings of oppression and misery, are by such men attained. With what increased force will this necessity apply to women? The absolute quantity of the time of confinement during life may not, on ordinary occasions, and under improved arrangements, be much: but the *tendency* to attach too great relative importance to domestic and selfish over social and sympathetic affections, to immediate over remote objects and enjoyments, must ever (if not by wise and benevolent expedients counteracted) remain with the sex which is from physical causes the most confined.

As the invention of gunpowder equalized the spirited man, though of weak muscular powers, with the strongest in mortal combat, so will the discovery of the system of representation and election extended to women, raise them above the physical inconveniences of their structure, and afford that counteracting attraction of a social and comprehensive nature, which is requisite to counterbalance the abuse by themselves and others of their occasionally unavoidable domestic occupations. It is with difficulty the mind is induced to occupy itself with that, though ever so conducive to general happiness, in which it has not direct obvious interest, or some mode of influence. Those only that have long cultivated the pleasures of intellectual processes and of the feelings of sympathy, spring with equal ardour to the comprehensive and the remote, the limited and the present, provided that preponderant happiness to those liable to be affected by it, is anticipated from the pursuit. Therefore to women as to men, and more than as to men, is the constant exercise of this check of political rights necessary. Without them, their attention would be lulled to rest: immediate domestic objects would, as now, engross all their care: the effects of regulations, over which they had no control, on their happiness, would be by them disregarded, uninquired into. As a miserable evasion for their incapacity of judging, they would gladly take up the plea, put into their mouths by their oppressors, that " such matters were no business of theirs." Equal civil and criminal laws, and an equal system of morals, would crumble to pieces, where knowledge was not constantly kept awake and interested in investigating the *consequences* of existing or proposed regulations. The power of electing and of being elected equally with men, wherever inclination and appropriate talent concurred, is the invigorating charm that would lead out the minds of women from an eternal association with mere childhood and childish toys, from isolation and stupidity, to high intercourse with minds of men equally cultivated and beneficent with their own, equally delighted to investigate with them all possible modes of producing human good, without deigning to inquire—what could never be resolved—which sex was most likely to be benefited by impartial justice. Nor would the education of children suffer by withdrawing the great majority of women, during the most useful periods of their lives, from being alternately their slaves or tyrants. On the contrary, their education would be inconceivably improved thereby. Children of nearly equal ages from many neighbouring families are the only proper companions for each other—happy and free creatures, exciting each other to thought and action, and awakening each other's sympathies. A superintendent only would be wanting, man or woman as may be most convenient, intelligent in the theory and practice of physical and mental culture, or if necessary both, surrounded with favorable circumstances merely, and thus giving an impulse to the developement of minds of hundreds indiscriminately of both sexes; or as children have been aptly termed, all of them of the *neutral* sex. Under our present uneconomical and vice- and misery-producing arrangements, nearly one half the human race is condemned to eternal childhood, to prevent from ever emerging from childhood the whole of the race. Few women, as now constituted, know how to form the disposition of a child for the first year of its life. One of the most important of human concerns is left every where to blind chance, to all the varieties of presumptuous ignorance. The audacity of pure ignorance in prescribing for the diseases of the bodies of children would be now universally reprobated; but the more pernicious audacity of prescribing for diseases of the mind, nay more, of ingrafting and nurturing them till they become sources of mischief to all around, is regarded with complacency from the almost universality of the practice. How long will parents be blind to their own and their children's improvement and happiness, both dependent on the same means of enlightened and beneficent culture? But under whatever system children are regulated, whether, as now, isolated with uncongenial minds and habits, or, as they ought to be, associated with numbers of similar ages, the necessity of enlargement of mind, for the right intellectual and moral developement of children, is not the less necessary in their instructors. Though rendered the more difficult of acquisition, such enlargement of mind is not the less indispensable, but the more so, in proportion to the greater difficulty of forming isolated characters: the greater the difficulty of the task, the greater ought to be the skill in order to perform it well. The more women are isolated and stultified with their children, with their fire and food-preparing processes, the more it is necessary, though the more difficult it becomes, that they should receive illumination and comprehensiveness of mind from without, in order to counterbalance this unfavorable tendency of their situation. The sharing equally in political rights with men, and thus acquiring an interest in what concerns others more than themselves, themselves in combination with others to the extent, sometimes, of the whole of mankind, is the only mode of curing the defects of character to which the organization of women renders them more prone than men, and which have a constant tendency to render them indifferent and inattentive to those remote circumstances and arrangements, those delicate agencies of laws and morals on which the possibility of acquiring happiness ultimately depends. In order to preserve an equal chance of happiness arising from an equal system of morals and equal civil and criminal laws, it is thus even more necessary for women than for men to maintain the check and the exercise of political rights.

Much pernicious mystification has been made use of by means of such phrases as " the folly of opposing nature," " the wisdom of following her dictates." The wisdom of following nature may generally be translated by the wisdom of adopting the opinion of the person using such phrases. Where this is not the case, the distinction is plain: follow the dictates of nature, call forth and improve her physical tendencies, where calculating all their effects, immediate and remote, on the agent and others, a preponderant portion of good is to be obtained. On the contrary, as in almost all inclinations of the senses, and as in the case before us, wherever unlimited indulgence would lead to preponderant evil, there those remote views of interest must be brought forward which are requisite to afford motives to the mind to resist these natural tendencies, to oppose such dictates of nature. Where the yielding to immediate inclination, or to nature as the phrase is, is attended with no ulterior mischief to the agent or others, it is the part of benevolence to feel pleasure and to delight in promoting the gratification of such natural inclinations.

Thus does it appear that no equal system of morals, that no equal system of laws, can be relied upon by women as affording them an equal chance of happiness, in proportion to their powers and faculties, natural or acquired, with men, if not accompanied and supported by equal political rights. Without them they can never be regarded by men as really their equals, they can never attain that respectability and dignity in the social scale, which would cause either the bona fide execution or the permanence of equal laws or equal morals. They could not respect themselves. All their blessings would hang on a straw, the continued good dispositions or good judgement of those whose immediate *apparent* interest must ever, under the system of exclusion, seem to be opposed to theirs. From the physical organization of women, and consequent greater tendency to domesticity and confinement than men, they must be more apt to undervalue the relative importance of the effects of distant and comprehensive regulations; whence the greater necessity of the check and exercise of political rights in them than even in men, in order to *counteract* this unfavorable tendency of circumstances to inattention to such matters. The possession of equal political rights, if not a complete check (because there can be no complete check on human inclinations and intellect, themselves imperfect), is the best the present state of knowledge affords on old habits of injustice and errors of judgement. Under the shield of free inquiry, the real interests of all would gradually be discovered, acknowledged, and practised.

Alas! the very imperfection of the check, though the

best or only one worthy of a thought that can be devised, is the real matter for regret. Timidity and inaptitude for a new species of exertion, arising from old habits of ignorance, submission, and degradation, would for a long time prevent women from judging for themselves, from regarding their happiness, so long ignorantly or perfidiously trampled under-foot, as equally entitled to respect with that of their stronger and bulkier associates. The physical power of constraint, of doing ill, possessed by men, must always operate, at least as long as the system of individual competition lasts, unknown to themselves, in cherishing a presumption of their own superior importance as the more powerful animals. Nothing but the gradual culture, till it shall become universal, of knowledge and benevolence will finally root out this baneful prejudice; though every improvement made every day, even in physical science and applied to the arts, is weakening the prejudice, by superseding the utility of brute force even for the supply of our most homely wants, and demonstrating the superior efficiency of scientific skill.

As society improves, and in proportion to its improvement, the respect paid to brute unconscious force or to muscular strength decreases. There are two causes acting at the same time, and concurring to produce this effect: the one is the comparative inefficiency of mere force to produce useful results, even in the production of articles of wealth, when compared with knowledge and skill applied through machinery; the other is the new class of pleasures, continually increasing and expanding over a larger portion of society, arising from intellectual culture. The employment of brute force in foreign war, and to so great an extent in supporting the machinery of government and enforcing the sanctions of criminal law, tends to keep up this declining respect for force; though even here, as society advances, criminal laws become more mild, and skill is every day superseding, even in war, the efficiency of mere force. For three fourths of the operations, professions, arts, trades, now carried on by men, the muscular strength of women, moderately developed by healthful physical education, would be abundantly sufficient: the fourth, requiring the greatest developement of strength, would naturally be conducted by those amongst men who excel in that quality, and who are generally deficient in inclination to intellectual pursuits. Qualities are estimated by their utility: mere force or strength is now, and will be every day, of less and less comparative importance with intellectual qualities, from the decreasing benefits to be derived from it. In point of fact, even now the most ill paid offices are those in which mere force is required: force is so common and brutish a quality, that when not joined with skill, or not necessary to self-defence or attack, it is used as a means of support or influence by those only who have not within their command any more influential or better remunerated qualities. While, as society advances in improvement, the beneficially productive power of force decreases, the pleasures arising from the cultivation of intellect rise into existence, increase in importance, and come to be pursued for their own sake: more delicate pleasures, those of sympathy combined with intelligence, and always spreading over a larger surface, replace the more coarse and boisterous pleasures of mere muscular exertion.

These favorable tendencies of civilization, proceeding from the decreased usefulness of mere force and from the new class of pleasures produced by mental culture, have doubtless mitigated the abuses of savage strength despotically used by man over woman. The progression of the same circumstances must doubtless in the end annihilate this abuse. Hitherto, though from these causes, the exercise of the domination has been in some countries becoming more mild, yet are the notions of superiority and the *power* of oppressing retained with almost as much pertinacity as ever. Superstition and an unequal and hypocritical system of morals, have erected the despotism of the one party into a right, and the submission of the other into a duty. The direct exercise of force is for the most part superseded by the previous drilling of the minds of the oppressors and the oppressed, the one as ready to bear, as the other to inflict, injustice. How long must it necessarily be, before these deep-rooted habitudes are eradicated ! how very long before the old and indirect influence of man over woman shall cease to modify and control to his own purposes the exercise of woman's newly acquired political rights ! How much is it to be dreaded, that until the education of truth and utility shall have raised the minds of both men and women, the influential party will render to a great extent inoperative the political rights of the other; and thus so far realize the taunts of those who predict the utter inefficiency of any checks, domestic, civil, or political, over the power of diminishing happiness and inflicting misery conferred by nature, in the gift of superior strength, on all those whom she has favored or, from its misuse cursed, with it.

We may rest then plainly and fully assured, that so far from the additional check of political rights being superfluous to women, to guaranty to them equal enjoyments proportioned to their faculties, under equal civil and criminal laws, the real cause of apprehension would be, that even the full possession of political rights would for a long time be but partially operative; and that to attain their full and salutary effects we must look forward to that time when the progress of knowledge and of new institutions shall have obliterated a prejudice coeval with the race of man, and in the early stages of his progress, previous to the developement of knowledge, impressed upon him by the very necessities of his existence. Political rights then are not only necessary to secure to women the existence of equal civil and criminal laws between them and men; but if it were possible to devise a check still more likely to be efficient to procure for them this demand of equal justice, that additional check ought to be employed.

The investigation being concluded of the three Questions proposed to be discussed, in reply to the last effort of philosophy, of the much abused philosophy of Utility, to cover with a mockery of pretended reason, an affectation of justice, the habitual and universal thraldom, and consequent privation of enjoyment and infliction of evil, physical, sympathetic, and intellectual, on one half the human race— what remains to be done? It cannot be expected that the general question of the expediency of improving equally the faculties of all human beings and affording an equal freedom of exertion for all on the great field of human competition or co-operation, in order to effect thereby an immense increase to the sum-total of human happiness, should be here discussed. Tempting and vast as the field is, overwhelming as would be the facts and reasonings in demonstrating the always concurrent ignorance and brutality of existing exclusions and usurpation of despotic power, triumphantly as they would establish the cause of the oppressed and degraded half of the race, they cannot here be entered into. Strictly speaking, the examination of our first question, namely, "Are the interests of women in point " of fact involved in those of men ?" was a sufficient reply to the paragraph in the " Article on Government." That monstrous assertion disproved, the whole fabric built upon it, necessarily falls to the ground. If the interests of women are not involved in those of men, the law ought to secure to them equal political rights : this is established by the reasoning of the " Article" itself. The discussion of the two last questions, therefore, were works of supererogation. Even so they may give an impulse to the minds of some of those who have been all their lives benumbed by the withering influence of an insolent domination, which, not satisfied with controlling the outward actions, withholds knowledge from the mind as well as physical developement from the body, and completes its odious work, not satisfied with mere ignorance and prostration of all the faculties of its victims, by inculcating submission to arbitrary will as a moral duty, and encompassing the slave with a superstitious horror of its own freedom.

Women of England! women, in whatever country ye breathe—wherever ye breathe, degraded—awake! Awake to the contemplation of the happiness that awaits you when all your faculties of mind and body shall be fully cultivated and developed; when every path in which ye can exercise those improved faculties shall be laid open and rendered delightful to you, even as to them who now ignorantly enslave and degrade you. If degradation from long habitude have lost its sting, if the iron have penetrated so deeply into your frame that it has been gradually taken up into the system and mingles unperceived amidst the fluids of your life; if the prostration of reason and the eradication of feeling have kept pace within you, so that you are insensible alike to what you suffer and to what you might enjoy,—your case were all but hopeless. Nothing less, then, than the sight presented before your eyes, of the superior happiness enjoyed by other women, under arrangements of perfect equality with men, could arouse you. Such a sight, even under such circumstances, would excite your envy and kindle up all your extinct desires. But you are not so degraded. The unvaried despotism of so many thousand years, has not so entirely degraded you, has not been able to extinguish within you the feelings of nature, the love of happiness and of equal justice. The united exertions of law, superstition, and pretended morals of past ages of ignorance, have not entirely succeeded. There is still a germ within you, the love of happiness, coeval with your existence, and never to cease but when " life itself shall please no more," which shall conduct you, feeble as it now is, under the guidance of wisdom and benevolence, to that perfect equality of knowledge, sympathy, and enjoyment with men, which the greatest sum of happiness for the whole race demands.

Sleeps there an infant on your bosom, to the level of whose intellect the systematic despotism and pitiful jealousy of man have not sought, and for the most part successfully sought, to chain down yours? Does no blush rise amongst you—swells no breast with indignation, at the enormous wrong? Simple as ye are, have ye become enamoured of folly? do you indeed believe it to be a source of power and of happiness? Look to your masters: does knowledge in their hands remain idle? is it with them no source of power and happiness? Think ye then indeed that it is of the use of what are called your personal charms alone that man is jealous? There is not a quality of mind which his animal propensities do not grudge you : not one, those only excepted which, like high-seasoned or far-fetched sauces, render you, as objects of sense, more stimulating to his purely selfish desires. Do ye pretend to enjoy with him, at this banquet of *bought* or *commanded* sensuality, the sensuality of prostitution or of marriage? He has a system of domineering hypocrisy, which he calls morals, which brands with the name of vice your enjoyment, while it lauds with the name of virtue, or gilds with that of innocent gratification, his. What quality, worth the possession, and capable of being applied to useful purposes for your own independence and happiness, do you possess, of which ignorant man is not jealous? Strength is his peculiar prerogative ; it is *unfeminine* to possess it: hence every expedient is used in what is called your education, to enervate your bodies, by proscribing that activity which is as necessary to health as to preservation from inevitable casualties. Muscular weakness, what is called delicacy of health approaching to disease, helplessness, are by a strange perversion of language denominated rather perfections than defects in women, in order to increase their dependence, even their *physical* dependence on man ; gratifying by one operation his two ruling animal propensities, sexual desire and love of domination. Hectic delicacy of health—though to yourselves accompanied by torment and followed by death—excites man's appetite; and utter weakness, no matter what personal evils it may entail on the possessor, gratifies his love of domination, by rendering his aid on every trivial occasion indispensable for your protection or for your most trifling exertions. Not satisfied with the inferiority of strength which your comparative size and structure, under the name of nature, give you, his poor jealousy increases it a hundredfold by all the resources of a vicious and partial physical training: and for this weakness and helplessness you are subsequently reproached, as a mark of your natural physical inferiority! Of strength of mind in you the ignorant amongst men, that is to say, the bulk of men, are still more jealous than of strength of body. Cowardice, that is to say, dread without reason, and in consequence of that dread, incapacity of using the means of preservation in your power against the most trifling attacks of the most contemptible animals or even insects or petty accidents, is by the sexual system of morality rather a virtue than a vice in you. No matter what inconveniences you personally suffer from this pernicious quality, no matter how your minds through life are tormented by it; it is of much more importance that man's vanity should be perfumed with his comparative hardihood than that you should be happy. Not on benevolence, but on antipathy, or malignant jealousy of your good, is the cursed system of sexual morality founded. Strength, without which there can be no health, both of body and mind, would cause you to approach too nearly to those high prerogatives in your masters, with whom to aim at an equality is the summit of female audacity, if not of wickedness. Prudence for the management of your affairs, wisdom for the guidance of your voluntary actions, the same unrelenting jealousy of ignorance proscribes. An education of baby-clothes, and sounds, and postures, you are given, instead of real knowledge; the *incidents* are withheld from you, by which you could learn, as man does, the management of affairs and the prudential guidance of your own actions; and thus factitiously incapacitated, man interposes, seizes on your property, leaves you none to manage, and assumes the despotic guidance of your actions, as the right of his superior wisdom and prudence! Every moral and intellectual quality of which you might be possessed, is thus deliberately and systematically sacrificed at the shrine of man's all-devouring jealousy, of his most immoral love of superiority, deriving pleasure where if benevolent he could not avoid feeling pain, from the contemplation of the weaknesses, vices, or privations, thus entailed upon you his fellow-creatures. That no intellectual faculties may be by you developed, it is *immoral* that you should exercise even the faculty of speech (though it is a quality at times of the highest virtue, exciting the utmost admiration in *man*), to address in public, that is to say, to address any where, numbers of your fellow-creatures; this high and exciting source of influence and intellectual improvement, man's universal jealousy having also monopolized. On the stage, as servants, as *despised* servants, you may act and receive his payment to flatter his eye and ear; but for your own interest in life, to turn to any serious use those powers of graceful and reasoning eloquence, which these illicit occasions have shown you to possess, and with which they have enabled you to thrill man's overpowered faculties, his cowardly and malignant jealousy forbids the exercise. An excluding law would be in th s case superfluous. Though superhuman wisdom were to be gleaned by woman, as grains from the well reaped fields of men, and in spite of their exclusions, your lips, the vehicle of such wisdom, would be closed, in spite of the vain permissions of law, by the superior strength of men, even by open force!

How can you be generous, how prove that you are beneficent? Man seizes for his own exclusive use the pecuniary means of generosity and beneficence. As daughters, as wives—a few rare cases excepted for trifling objects—you have no more command of property to gratify those propensities, than the children which you are the passive machines of producing. Even if you had these means, are not almost all of what ought to be your voluntary actions, under the control of others? Without voluntariness of action, can there be any morality? The power of judging of matters of extensive usefulness, and the means of making that judgement available to good, are alike withheld from you. Every good quality that can command the respect of others, that can procure influence in society, that can procure personal benefit to the possessor, man reserves to himself, and from the possession of them he carefully excludes you. Whatever qualities tend to make you objects of greater attraction to man's two great ruling passions regarding you, love of sensual pleasure, love of domination, he permits, he commands you to cultivate. Beauty, cleanliness, grace, obedience, modesty. O, yes! be cleanly, be graceful, be obedient, be modest; be modest of yourselves, of your own merits; blush without reason through mere ignorance; be humble to abjectness, that you may swell man's stupid pride by vour adulation and acknowledged immeasurable inferiority! Whatever qualities again encroach the least upon, or tend to accumulate, his means of sensual gratification, of avarice, influence, or ostentatious display—such qualities as temperance, thriftiness, devotedness to his interest—he permits you to possess. All these are useful to *him*, to his love of sense, of power, of wealth. But whatever qualities are useful to *yourselves alone*, whatever qualities do not tend to retain you, creatures subordinate merely and tributary to his happiness, whatever qualities excite the admiration and sympathy of others ; these, in you, man's sexual system of morality condemns. He sneers and calls these qualities *unfeminine*—a word, in its ordinary moral application, of supreme folly, which merely means that he does not wish that you should possess these qualities,—but attempts not to show that they are not of extreme utility to the possessors. Wherever laws do not, directly or indirectly, by exclusions or punishments, interfere, to render the attainment or the exercise of such qualities impracticable, superstition and public opinion are called in by man to his aid, and future terrors and present privations and persecutions attend the hardihood of those few amongst women who (personal wealth not having, by rare accident, made them independent) presume to covet the possession and the exercise of such qualities, as would put them on an equality, in point of moral and intellectual influence, and in point of happiness of every species, with men. Thus degraded to the level of mere automatons, the passive tools of the pleasures and passions of men, your actions are regulated, like those of automatons or slaves, by the arbitrary will of masters, to whom, by the necessities of existence uniting yourselves, you are compelled to vow uninquiring obedience. O wretched slaves of such wretched masters!

Awake, arise, shake off these fetters. Acquire the mental power of seeing them, and they are loosened for ever. Their magic depends on your ignorance, on your submission. Fear not that such chains can by remonstrance, by rebellion, be rendered more severe. Can human being be sunk lower in degradation than, though possessed of the capacity of acquiring the intellect and benevolence of fabled superior powers, to be liable in every action to the arbitrary command of another human being, that human being ever so vile? pleasures to be meted out, friendships, acquaintances, to be *permitted?* walks, goings-in and goings-out to be regulated or prohibited? pursuits to be prescribed? nay, restraint and blows to be inflicted as on helpless children? A Madame Roland—the slave of a hangman, should chance marry her to such a one, or to a worse fiend than a hangman though in better dress! And men pleasantly tell you to be patient, to continue submissive, lest these chains should be rendered more galling. That they are not more galling is entirely owing to man's calculation of his own interest, not of your happiness. A woman's happiness in man's scale of sexual morality!—unmeaning hypocrisy! For *his own sake* man is restrained; he dare not, he cannot, render your chains more galling. Himself the slave of sensual pleasure, he wishes to enjoy it with the most pleasing accompaniments. Your frowns and active hatred, the inevitable result of his perseverance in persecution, would mar his banquet of sensuality : it would paralyse your expected activity of meretricious blandishments, to heighten his selfish unparticipated joy.

Submission!—have you not since the records of the race been submissive? Of what avail, your thousands of years of submission! that at the end of it, in a country calling itself the most enlightened in civilization, by an advocate of the latest and most enlightened system of philosophy, the glorious principle of Utility itself, hardly born, is prostituted to seal your eternal degradation, classing you with the immature, imperfectly developed portion of the human race, with infants and children, to be governed at the arbitrary command of your masters! What slaves, since the accursed and accursing system of slavery began, have ever gained by contentment, by submission? If the slaves are pleased with their lot, why should their masters meditate a change? Can an argument, addressed to creatures so low in intellect—not to sully the name of benevolence by conjoining it with such beings—as to find delight in being slave-masters, be conceived more calculated to banish from their minds all notions of amelioration? Nay, nay: you must be soothed and gratified to deck with smiles man's sensual banquet : he is now forced to gratify your preposterous desires of capricious folly, engendered by his system of despotic control. Why not gratify your desires of wisdom and justice, at a *less expense,* and attended with overwhelming benefits to the whole human race? To be free, women, that is to say, all women, like all men, have only to desire it, to perceive their real interest, always harmonizing with the interest of the whole race, and fearlessly to advocate it. Demand with mild but unshrinking firmness, perfect equality with men : demand equal civil and criminal laws, an equal system of morals, and, as indispensable to these, equal political laws, to afford you an equal chance of happiness with men, from the developement and exercise of your faculties, in that open field of competition in which nature has given to men the advantage of superior physical strength.

Whatever system of labor, that by slaves or that by freemen; whatever system of government, that by one, by a few, or by many, have hitherto prevailed in human society; under every vicissitude of MAN'S condition, he has always retained woman his slave. The republican has exercised over you that hateful spirit of domination which his fellow man and citizen disdained to submit to. Of all the sins and vices of your masters, you have been made the scapegoats: they have enjoyed, and you have suffered for their enjoyments; suffered for the very enjoyments of which they compel you to be the instruments! What wonder that your sex is indifferent to what man calls the progress of society, of freedom of action, of social institutions? Where amongst them all, amongst all their past schemes of liberty or despotism, is the freedom of action *for you?* Slaves every where, and to all alike: but strange to say, least enslaved (except to the common masters of both male and female slaves) under the very system of slavery itself: there, the children of the whole population being with an equal degree of discomfort provided for by the master, and the labor of women in rearing children being equally recompensed with that of other slave labor, female slaves are not under the necessity of becoming a second time the individualized slaves of their male companions in wretchedness, to be by them supported. And men wonder at your indifference to high matters of liberty and human weal! Is their folly or their hypocrisy the greater?

To obtain equal rights, the basis of equal happiness with men, you must be *respected* by them; not merely desired, like rare meats, to pamper their selfish appetites. To be respected by them, you must be respectable in your own eyes; you must exert more power, you must be more useful. You must regard yourselves as having equal capabilities of contributing to the general happiness with men, and as therefore equally entitled with them to every enjoyment. You must exercise these capabilities, nor cease to remonstrate till no more than equal duties are exacted from you, till no more than equal punishments are inflicted upon you, till equal enjoyments and equal means of seeking happiness are permitted to you as to men.

Still evils encompass you, inherent in the very system of labor by individual competition, even in its most free and perfect form. Men dread the competition of other men, of each other, in every line of industry. How much more will they dread your additional competition! How much will this dread of the competition of your industry and talents be aggravated by their previous contempt of your fabricated impotence! Hard enough, now, they will say, to earn subsistence and to acquire comforts: what will it be when an additional rivalship, equal to perhaps one third of actual human exertion, is thrown into the scale against them? How fearfully would such an influx of labor and talents into the market of competition bring down their remuneration!

An evil of no less magnitude, and immediately consequent on the preceding, opposes your happiness in the present state of social arrangements. Will man, laboring by individual competition, afford you any part of the fruits of his individual exertions as a compensation for the loss of time, pain, and expense incurred by women in bearing and rearing his and your common children? His present compensation of measured food, clothing, and idleness, with despotism over young children and inferior animals to compensate for his more lofty despotism over yourselves, coupled with personal insignificance, in what he calls his marriage contract, you know, or ought to know, how to appreciate. But not to say that this can only apply to that portion amongst you whom necessity compels to enter into so iniquitously partial a yoke; not to say that the duties and enjoyments of marriage might, if man ceased to be an ignorantly selfish creature, be rendered equal to both the contracting parties; the utmost compensation you could expect from this source would never afford you a permanent chance of happiness equal to that of men. You will always, under the system of individual competition and individual accumulations of wealth, be liable to the casualty of misery on the death of the active producer of the family, and occasional injustice from domestic abuse of superior strength and influence, against which no laws can entirely guard. Under the system of production by individual competition, it is impossible to expect that public opinion should be raised so high as to supply the defects of law, which can only repress—at the expense of the minor evils of punishment—the more flagrant and proveable acts of injustice, but can not take cognizance of those minute occurrences which so often form the groundwork of the happiness or misery of life. Superiority in the production or accumulation of individual wealth will ever be whispering into man's ear preposterous notions of his relative importance over woman, which notions must be ever prompting him to unsocial airs towards women, and particularly towards that woman who co-operates with him in the rearing of a family: for, individual wealth being under this system the one thing needful, all other qualities not tending to acquire it, though contributing ever so largely to increase the common stock of mutual happiness, are disregarded; and compensation for the exercise of such qualities or talents, for the endurance of pains and privations, would scarcely be dreamed of. If man, pursuing individual wealth, condescend to be equally instrumental with you in the production of children, the whole of the pleasure he takes care to enjoy and make the most of, as his by right of superior strength; but as to the pains and privations which his enjoyments may have entailed upon another, where is the bond that his labor should afford compensation for them?

Not so under the system of, Association, or of Labor by Mutual Co-operation.

This scheme of social arrangements is the only one which will complete and for ever insure the perfect equality and entire reciprocity of happiness between women and men. Those evils, which neither an equality of civil and criminal laws, nor of political laws, nor an equal system of morals upheld by an enlightened public opinion, can entirely obviate, this scheme of human exertion will remove or abundantly compensate. Even for the partial dispensations of nature it affords a remedy. Large numbers of men and women co-operating together for mutual happiness, all their possessions and means of enjoyment being the equal property of all—individual property and competition for ever excluded—women are not asked to *labor* as much in point of strength of muscle as men, but to contribute what they can, with as much cheerful benevolence, to the common happiness. All talents, all faculties, whether from nature or education, whether of mind or muscle, are here equally appreciated if they are spontaneously afforded and improved, and if they are necessary to keep up the common mass of happiness. Here no dread of being deserted by a husband with a helpless and pining family, could compel a woman to submit to the barbarities of an exclusive master. The whole Association educate and provide for the children of all: the children are independent of the exertions or the bounty of any individual parent: the whole wealth and beneficence of the community support woman against the enormous wrong of such casualties: they affect her not. She is bound by no motives to submit to injustice: it would not, therefore, be practised upon her. Here the evil of losing, by any accident, a beloved companion, is not aggravated to woman by the unanticipated pressure of overwhelming want. All her comforts, her respectability, depending on her personal qualities, remain unchanged: she co-operates as before to the common happiness, and her intelligent and sympathizing associates mitigate and gradually replace the bitterness of a last separation from the friend of her affections. Here, the daughter of the deserted mother could not, from want or vanity, sell the use of her person. She is as fully supplied with all comforts as any other member of the community, co-operating with them in whatever way her talents may permit to the common good. The vile trade of prostitution, consigning to untimely graves the youth and beauty of every civilized land, and gloated on by men pursuing individual wealth and upholding the sexual and partial system of morals, could not here exist. Man has, here, no individual wealth more than woman, with which to buy her person for the animal use of a few years. Man, like woman, if he wish to be beloved, must learn the art of pleasing, of benevolence, of deserving love. Here, the happiness of a young woman is not blasted for life by the scorn and persecutions of unrelenting hypocrisy, for that very indiscretion which weaves the gay chaplet of exulting gallantry round the forehead of unrestrained man. Morality is, here, just and equal in her awards. Why so? Because, man having no more wealth than woman, and no more influence over the general property, and his superior strength being brought down to its just level of utility, he can procure no sexual gratification but from the voluntary affection of woman: in proscribing her indiscretions, therefore, he must proscribe his own; and as far as the greatest degree of common happiness might require that such indiscretions should be equally repressed in the two sexes, so far and no farther would they be impartially discouraged in both. If women cease to be dependent on individual men for their daily support, if the children of all the pairs of the community are educated and maintained out of the common stock of wealth and talents, if every possible aid of medical skill and kindness is afforded impartially to all, to compensate for the bitterness of those hours when the organization of woman imposes on her superfluous sufferings; what motives, under such circumstances, could lead women to submit to unmerited reproach more than men, for those very acts in which men must from the very nature of things be equal participators? *No means of persecution being left to men,* all reproach not founded on reason and justice, all attempt at exclusive reproach, would be thrown back with laughter and contempt on the fools who harboured them. Woman's love must, under such circumstances be earned, be merited, not, as now, *bought* or *commanded:* it would not be prostituted on heartless miscreants who could first steal the gem and then murder with their scorn its innocent confiding owner. Such men, in such an Association, might love themselves! a species of love, in which they would find no rivals to molest them!

All sexual morality, and its attendant horrors of human misery, thus banished from these happy abodes of equal justice by the inevitable operation of circumstances, withdrawing the old, and affording new, motives to human exertion and judgement, the education of women being as comprehensive and useful as that of men, the inequality of chances of enjoyment to women, under the system of individual competition from average inequality of powers, being obviated, and all the compensation that human skill and kindness can afford being provided against the inevitable evils of nature or accident; what remains but that you should every where advocate, first, that partial equality which is all that equal laws, political and civil, equal morals, and an equal system of education can give you under the scheme of isolated individual, or family, exertion, now prevalent, and that you should also advocate, with an energy not inferior, the new social system of the Association of large numbers, all cheerfully contributing their exertions, muscular or mental, to the common good, and all equal in duties, rights, and enjoyments; the happiness of both men and women raised a hundredfold beyond what it now is? The scheme of Association or Mutual Co-operation, where all useful talents and efforts for the common good will be equally appreciated and rewarded, is the true haven for the happiness of both sexes, particularly of women. All motives are here taken away from men to practise injustice; all motives are taken away from women to submit to injustice. The practice of it will not, therefore, be attempted. As long as the exclusive individual possession of wealth remains the moving-spring of human society, so long will your peculiar pains and privations be disregarded and unrequited, and man will avail himself of his natural advantages of strength and uninterrupted exertion to exact an indirect domination over woman in the secrecy of domestic life, though laws and public opinion were opposed to such usurpation. It is not in human nature, possessed of power and the means of exercising it, and acting in every thing by individual competition, to abstain on all occasions from the abuse of that power. By Mutual Co-operation of large numbers, the power and the means of exercising it, and the desire of exercising it, are equally withdrawn. Women are here no more dependent on men, or on any individual man, than men are on women. Let the laws of general society be what they may, let them remain ever so brutal, even as they now are, respecting what they are pleased to term the marriage contract, no woman in these Associations of large numbers for mutual happiness, will be under any necessity, will find any possible motive, that could induce her to become the self-devoted slave to the caprices, or, capricious or not, to the *will* of any other human being. Cheerfully co-operating by personal exertion of mind, skill, or muscle, to the common good, possessing influence proportioned to her powers of reason and useful talent, sharing equally all benefits, watched over in sickness and health by equal care, what premium under such circumstances has man to offer to woman that she should be his slave in any thing ? No more than woman has to offer to man that he should be the slave of her appetites and capricious jealousies. Who wishes, man or woman, in these Communities to be esteemed or loved, must deserve to be esteemed or loved, and must look forward to the loss of love or esteem with the loss, or the neglect to practise, those good qualities which called esteem or love into existence. No persecution could here be practised to constrain the semblance, the mockery, of esteem or love when the reality had ceased to exist. To enjoy equal happiness with men, to associate with them on terms of perfect equality, you must be equally useful to the common good by an equal improvement and equally useful application of all your faculties of mind and body, in exchange for the state of domestic drudgery, ignorance, and insignificance to which you are now reduced, with various shades, in civilized as well as savage life. Then shall you and men salute each other with a real and mutual modesty, founded on mutual benevolence, on a just estimate of your several characters, and a knowledge of the mutual dependence of each on the other to elicit the highest degree of happiness; not, as now, with an air of superiority and condescending bounty on the one side, and on the other with downcast eyes, the willing and ignorant slaves of men's pampered and brutalizing appetites*.

---

* While Mr. Owen was in Scotland, at New Lanark, practically experimenting on the principles of the new Social System of Mutual Co-operation, a French writer, M. Charles Fourier (with whose eccentricities of speculation we are not here concerned) was studying the same subject at Lyons. As the result of the observations and meditations of 30 years, he has published in Paris two large volumes, which he calls a " *Treatise of Industrial Association.*" In the great leading features of the Co-operation of large numbers for the production of wealth and social happiness, and the improved, and in-

Under such arrangements, women may have equal improvement and use of all their faculties with men: under these circumstances, they may derive as much of happiness from every source—of the senses, of intelligence, and sympathy—as men, according to the peculiarities of organization of each: under these circumstances, all may be perfectly equal in rights, duties, and enjoyments, according to their capabilities of acting, suffering, and enjoying. If men from an average superiority of strength, be able to add more to general happiness in the way of increasing the products of labor, where would happiness, where would men be found, were it not for the peculiar pains, privations and cares which women suffer in nourishing and rearing the infancy of the whole race? Against the almost doubtful advantage, in the present state of improved chemical and mechanical science and art, of mere superiority of animal strength on the part of men, in increasing their utility or contributions to the common happiness, may not the unquestionable usefulness of the employment of that part of the time of women which is consumed in preserving the race be opposed? Which more indispensable for human happiness, that a few more broadcloths or cottons should be every year produced, or that the race

---

dustrious, and *equal* education of *all* the children, Fourier agrees with Mr. Owen. But *inequality of distribution* is a leading feature of Fourier's system of Co-operation; while *equality* of distribution of wealth, as of all the means of happiness, seems to be the ultimate object of Owen's. Under the systems of both, under all systems of just Co-operation, not only will equal protection of Institutions be granted to women with men, but equal means of happiness from all sources will be insured to them.

itself should be every year increased and kindly and skilfully nurtured? Wherever the principle of Association prevailed, justice would prevail, and these mutual compensations—as nurturing infants against strength—would be fully admitted; no person cheerfully exerting his or her means, whatever they might be, for the common benefit, would be punished for the scantiness of those means, still less for the pains or privations attending their developement. In this, as in all the other arrangements of Mutual Co-operation, the punishments of nature, whether arising from decrease of enjoyments or from positive pain, would not only perhaps be found sufficient for all useful purposes, but would rather demand compensation than factitious increase.

But in a state of society where these compensations are not allowed, where man's advantage of superior strength is heightened by every possible means, rendered more effective by a monopoly of knowledge and fenced round by exclusive privileges; where woman's peculiar efforts and powers for the common benefit of the race are looked upon as an additional badge of inferiority and disgrace; where, instead of *compensation* for physical suffering and care useful to the whole race, such inconveniences, joined to those of inferior strength, are aggravated by every possible brutal contrivance of forced ignorance and exclusion from almost all the means of wealth and influence, pleasure and improvement; where man, for the exercise of his peculiar talent, strength, attended naturally in its developement with pleasure, rewards himself with every factitious benefit within the reach of his strength, and, amongst other apparent benefits, with the subjection of one half his species; while woman for the exercise of her peculiar faculty or talent, the bearing and nurture of infants, equally the independent gift of nature, but attended in its developement with pain, privation, and care, instead of being rewarded, as man is for his natural advantage of strength, is punished, the helplessness of suffering being made the basis of still further degradation ; where the generality of men, educated in brutal ignorance of the art of social happiness, seek for no higher pleasures from their intercourse with women than the gratification of the mere animal feeling of selfish appetite, and the still viler pleasure of mere despotic control over the objects of that appetite, and the children which it may be instrumental in producing;—in such a state of things you may well doubt that the mere removal of partial sexual restraints would raise woman to an equality with man. Many as are the years during which the Catholics of Ireland have been eligible to some few corporation and other offices, but very few of them have been so elected, because *the keys of admission were absurdly or perfidiously left in the hands of the exclusionists.* So must it in some measure be with the removal of the partial legislation and partial morals affecting women. Men, from their acquired advantages, must be every where the executors and judges—for a long time at least—under the new regulations, themselves parties or sympathizing with the parties in every cause.

In the mean time, however, until the association of men and women in large numbers for mutual benefit shall supersede the present isolated mode of exertion by individual competition, assert every where your right as human beings to equal individual liberty, to equal laws, political, civil, and criminal, to equal morals, to equal education,— and, as the result of the whole, to equal chances, according to the extent and improvement of your faculties and exertions, of acquiring the means of happiness, with men. Immense would be the accession of happiness to both men and women by such a change, though it should still leave uncompensated those casualties, attended with pain and privation to you individually, but of the very highest order of utility to the whole race, to which you are exclusively subjected. The removal of all *partial* existing restraints of law or custom, and the unfolding of the career of equal exertion to women and men, instead of being any obstacle to your further advancement under the system of Mutual Co-operation, would be the most certain step in the progress towards it, would prepare you to perceive its benefits, and render you anxious on the first opportunity to embrace them. No wretches ever passed from a state of slavery to a state of freedom without more or less of mental excitement, without more or less of alarm to the timid amongst their masters. These are partial and necessary evils, swelling almost into blessings from the immensity of preponderant good by which they are followed. Regard them not. Truth, benevolence, the interest of the whole human race, are on your side. Persevere, and you must be free. If to your intelligence and efforts this mighty change in human affairs shall be indebted, you will lay men under an obligation of gratitude to you, in comparison with which the past use of your mere animal charms would be like the fretful dream of the morning.

Nor will your fellow-creatures, men, long resist the change. They are too deeply concerned to continue long to oppose what palpably tends to their happiness: they are too deeply concerned not to be compelled to re-consider the barbarous systems of law and morals under which they have been brought up. In justice, in pity to them, submit no longer ; no longer *willingly* submit to their caprices. Though your bodies may be a little longer kept in servitude, degrade not yourselves by the repetition of superfluous vows of obedience : cease to kiss the rod : let your *minds* be henceforth free. The morn of loosening your physical chains will not be far distant.

Wretched as is, as has always been, your political, civil, domestic, and individual position—what reason have you to believe it likely to be improved without the energetic co-operation of your own exertions, without your own unshrinking determination ?

Mark the effect on human character of that system of education pursued at all our public seminaries, exclusively devoted as they are to the males of our race. Can the tiger passions, so sedulously cultivated in our youths at their public schools, to be hereafter exercised on their fellow-men, give any promise of more kindly treatment to your sex, who are so entirely in their power, in whose favor no restraint of law exists, no punishment for injury, exceptindeed the deadly blow be given—though even then a loop-hole of retreat can be found for the murderer ? Arouse ! awake ! rescue your sex, your species, from the frightful circumstances that surround and degrade you : —demand your rights ; or man, ungenerous man, intoxicated with his power, may become still more presumptuous, and no longer measure or calculate the effect of his actions towards you, relying on your apathetic submission, while improvement in every other department of human exertion is on the advance.

Behold our youths brought up in the indulgence of all the cruel and ferocious passions, as inimical to the developement of the higher intellectual faculties as they are revolting to reason and humanity—sad proof of the shortsighted ignorance of their teachers! Behold them hence taught, nay compelled to believe, that all who want force to oppose to theirs, are by nature made over to them as objects of oppression, of sport, and contempt.

Demand then with confidence and dignity your portion of the common rights of all:—assume the high post that nature has assigned you; become the respectable and respected mothers and instructors of men; arrest this education of brutality; and cease to be the mere degraded instruments of men's sensual pleasures.

Do not those male portions of the human race who are oppressed by their fellow-men, occasionally see and feel their wrongs? Do they not occasionally break in upon the debasing slumbers of their foolish and wretched oppressors, by communing about their wrongs, by remonstrating and petitioning for their removal?

When will you, the most oppressed and degraded of the human race—for no vice, for no crime degraded and oppressed—see your wrongs, commune about them, break in upon the leaden slumbers of your masters, and remonstrate and petition for their removal? When will you remonstrate and demand that the same enlarged education, which ought to be afforded to all men, should also be afforded to you? that all exclusive laws restraining your exertions should be repealed? that your persons, in whatever situation in life, should be equally protected from *assault*, imprisonment, or restraint of any kind, with those of men? that, whether married or not, your actions, like those of men, should be regulated by your own notions of propriety and duty, restrained only by equal and just laws? that the same punishments, whether legal or moral, and no more than the same punishments, should be awarded to you, for the same vices or crimes, that are to men awarded? and that the same political and civil rights that men enjoy should be secured to you, because from the comparative want of strength you are more in need than men, of such legal protection?

The slow advance that man makes in obtaining his own liberties is a proof of what is called the retributive justice of nature, or the unerring tendency of injustice to produce accumulated evils. He wishes to obtain liberty for himself; yet selfishly conspires to exclude from its blessings one half his race. What is man, that he can pretend to change these tendencies, and produce two contrary effects—your degradation and his own happiness—by means not only inadequate, but opposed to the nature of things and to each other?

Shall he obtain liberty and happiness for himself, whilst resolved to deny it to the other half of his species? Can he ever become consistently just to his fellow-creature man, whilst he remains uniformly unjust to his fellow-creature woman? No, no; the principle of justice must be equal in its operation, extending to the whole human family, before men can reasonably hope any result from their labors, but that self-delusion which mocks them with an *ideal advance,* whilst yet chained down by their oppression of you to misery, vice, and eternally recurring disappointment.

O woman, from your auspicious hands may the new destiny of your species proceed! The collective voices of your sex raised against oppression will ultimately make men themselves your advocates and debtors. Reflect then seriously on your miserable and degraded position—your youth, your beauty, your feelings, your opinions, your actions, your time, your few years' fever of meritricious life —all made tributary to the appetites and passions of men. Whatever pleasures you enjoy, are permitted you for man's sake. Nothing is your own; protection of person and of property are alike withheld from you. Nothing is yours, but secret pangs, the bitter burning tears of regret, the stifled sobs of outraged nature thrown back upon your own hearts, where the vital principle itself stands checked, or is agitated with malignant passions, until body and mind become the frequent prey to overwhelming disease; now finding vent in sudden phrensy, now plunged in pining melancholy, or bursting the weak tenement of reason, seeking relief in self-destruction.

How many thousand of your sex *daily* perish thus unpitied and unknown; often victims of pressing want, always of privation and the arbitrary laws of heartless custom; condemned to cheerless solitude, or an idiot round of idle fashionable pursuits; your morning of life perhaps passed by, and with it the lingering darling hope of sympathy expired—puppets once of doting ignorant parents, whose tenderness for you outlived not your first youth; who, careless of your future fate, "launched you into life without an oar," indigent and ignorant, to eat the tear-steeped bread of dependence as wives, sisters, hired mistresses or unpitied prostitutes! This is the fate of the many, nay, of all your sex, subject only to those shades of difference arising from very peculiar circumstances or the accident of independent fortune; though even here the general want of knowledge, withheld from your sex, keeps even those individuals who are favored by fortune bowed to the relentless yoke which

Misery arising from their degraded situation.

man's laws, his superstitions, and hypocritical morality, have prepared for you.

For once then instruct man in what is good, wash out the foul stain, equally disgraceful to both sexes—that your sex has unbounded influence in making men to do evil, but cannot induce them to do good.

How many Thaises are there, who, vain of the empire they hold over the passions of men, exercise at all risks this contemptible and pernicious influence—the only influence permitted them—in stimulating these masters of the world to destroy cities; and, regardless of the whispers of conscience and humanity, often shake men's tardy resolutions to repair the evils they have caused!—Shall none be found with sufficient knowledge and elevation of mind to persuade men to do good, to make the most certain step towards the regeneration of degraded humanity, by opening a free course for justice and benevolence, for intellectual and social enjoyments, by no colour, by no sex to be restrained? As your bondage has chained down man to the ignorance and vices of despotism, so will your liberation reward him with knowledge, with freedom and with happiness.

THE END.

INDEX.

A.

Abjectness, 192.
Absurdities, 103.
Accidents, 190.
Activity, or Active Talent, 135, 139.
Address to Women, 187.
Adulation, 192.
Advance, ideal, 211.
Advantages, vii. 207.
Advocates, ix. 211.
Alarm, 208.
Alchemy, 11.
Alleviation, 130.
Anathema, vii.
Animals, 96, 183, 190.
Antipathy, 94, 96, 97, 138, 156, 160, 190.
Appeal, viii. 1.
Appetites, xii. 204, 212.
Aptitude, moral, 40, 60, 128, 135.
——— intellectual, 135, 146.
Argument, 1, 182.
Arrangements, 199.
"Article on Government," vii. xiv. 3, 4, 5, 6, 9, 16, 19, 25, 34, 36, 42, 50, 52, 54, 58, 75, 78, 96, 98, 107, 108, 109, 116, 117, 120, 124, 170.
Aspasia, 60.
Assaults, 88, 210.
Association, voluntary, ix. xii. 151, 199, 204, 206, 207.
Automatons, 193.
Avarice, 193.

B.

Baby-clothes, 205.
Barbary, piratical states, 68.
Bars, 156.
Basis, 196.
Beauty, vi. 192, 200, 212.
Benevolence, 123, 133, 192, 208, 213.
Bentham, viii. 3, 9.
Blacks, 97.
Blush, 189, 192.
Bondage, 213.
Boon, 208.
Breeding establishments, 104.
British India, 3, 8.
Broadcloths, 205.
Brutes, 70.

C.

Capability, 136.
Caprice, 99, 170, 209.
Casualties, 208.
Catholics, 207.
Chains, 194, 209.
Character, 64, 122, 123, 209.
Charms, 208.
Check, 134, 172, 177, 180, 182.
Children, x. 10, 12, 14, 16, 17, 18, 80, 179, 180.
Circumstances, 12, 13, 28, 38, 39, 40, 57, 177.
Civilization, 184, 86.
Claims of women, 159, 195.
Cleanliness, 192.
Clothing, 197.
Code of marriage, x. xiii. (See Marriage.)

Command, 43.
Community, 200.
Companion, 200.
Compensation, x. xi. 197, 206.
Competition, vi. 32, 34, 149, 156, 157, 162, 197, 198.
Comprehensiveness of view, iii. 131, 164, 169.
Conduct, 170.
Confinement, 177.
Consequences, 179.
Constituents, 176.
Contempt, 80, 197.
Contentment, 101.
Contract, (see Marriage) 55, 56.
Control, 44, 73, 192.
Conversation, v.
Conviviality, 77.
Co-operation, ix. xii. 151, 199, 204, 209.
Cottons, 205.
Counterpoise, 132.
Courage, vii. 140, 141.
Cowardice, 190.
Crime, 171.

D.

Danger, 184.
Daughters, adult, 21, 27, 34—53, 72, 192.
Dedication, vi.
Definition of a slave, 66.
Degradation, v. 19, 62, 194, 103, 167, 211.
Demands, or claims, of women, 159, 195.
Desires, 64.
Despotism, 9, 15, 43, 47, 62, 64, 70, 87, 91, 106, 213.
Developement, 206.
Devotedness, 193.
Difference, 69.
Discoverers, 137.
Diseases, 142, 180, 212.
Display, 193.

Distribution of wealth, 46, 205.
Divisions, of women, three, 27, 34, 54.
Domesticity, 177, 180.
Domination, 192.
Dream, 208.
Drilling, 185.
Drudgery, vii. 204.
Dumont, Mr., of Geneva, viii.
Duties, 167, 197.

E.

Education, xiii. 80, 161, 179, 185, 191, 209.
Election, 177.
Elephants, 120.
Eligibility, 164.
Eloquence, 191.
Encyclopædia Britannica (Supplement), vii. 3, 5, 40.
England, 187.
Englishman, 7, 16.
Enjoyments, 38, 39, 62, 76, 77, 80, 82, 97, 103, 151, 155, 156, 158, 197, 200, 213.
Envy, 108.
Epicurism, 77.
Equality of improvement and happiness, xiii. 96, 188, 195. 204.
———— of wealth, 205.
Equals, 17, 163.
Error of " Article," 28.
Europe, 15.
Exception, 9.
Exclusion of women, 14, 19, 25, 28, 79 to 93, 116, 159.
Exclusionists, 207.
Expense, 195.
Experience, 58.

F.

Faculties, 159, 191, 199, 206.
Falsehood, 17, 19, 62, 107, 171.
Family, 49.
Fathers, 9, 27, 34—53, 75.

Fellow-creatures, 208.
Fidelity, 61, 78.
Folly, 189, 196.
Food, 197.
Force, 17, 54, 141, 183, 184.
Fortitude, 140.
Fortune, 212.
Fourier, 204.
Fourth of the human race 174.
Freedom, 157, 208,2 13.

G.

Gallantry, 201.
Gauntlet, viii.
Gem, 202.
Generosity, 192.
Geneva, viii. 3.
Genius, 136.
Germ, 188.
Gestation, x. 123, 136, 142.
Governing by division, 131.
Government, 183, 196.
——————— self, 47.
Grace, 192.
Gratification, 89, 182.
Gratitude, 208.
Graves, 200.
Guarantee, ix. 166, 184.

H.

Habits, 206.
Half the human race, 4, 7, 19.
Hangman, 194.
Happiness, xiii. 4, 7, 13, 27, 45, 69, 73, 91, 92, 101, 107, 119, 208, 209, 213.
Hardihood, 193.
Hays, Mary, viii.
Health, 76, 189.
Highwayman, 29.
Hindostan, 3, 92.
Horror, 187.
Human beings, xiv. 7, 207.
Husbands, x. 9, 54—107, 161, 162, 172.
Hypocrisy, v. ix. 38, 78, 88, 106, 125, 143, 170, 171, 189, 196.

Hypothesis, 150.

I.

Idleness, 197.
Ignorance, 51, 74, 194.
Imbecillity, 81.
Immorality, 79.
Impediments, xi.
Imperfection, 182.
Imprisonment, 67, 68, 79, 85, 122.
Improvement, 151, 183
Impunity, 167, 172.
Incapacity, 164.
Incidents, 122, 135, 191
Inclinations, 181, 182.
Indissolubility, xiii. 56.
Industry, 157.
Inefficiency, 185.
Inequality, xiii. 56, 77, 205.
Infancy, 205.
Infant, 188.
Inference, 4,
Inferiority, 164, 192.
Infidelity, 78, 163.
Influence, 193.
Injustice, 19.
Inquisitors, 171.
Insects, 190.
Insincerity, 168.
Institutions, 186, 205.
Instructors, 210.
Instruments, 196, 210.
Insult, 72.
Interest, v.
——————— identity of, 18, 21, 26.
Interpreter, vii.
Introduction to morals and legislation, 3.
Invention, 136.
Investigation, 186.
Involving of interests, 17, 27, 45 —52, 76, 98, 107, 113, 114.
Ireland, 207.

J.

Jealousy, 188, 190, 192.

Judgement, 174, 176.
Justice, 126, 161, 164, 195, 209, 211, 213.
Justification, 117.

K.

Knowledge, xiii. 34, 183, 213.

L.

Labor, 196, 199.
Lanark, New, 204.
Laws of human nature, 6, 7, 13.
—— of England, 45, 87, 88, 155, 160, 162, 164, 166, 168, 170, 172, 174, 184, 213.
Legislation of women, 127—151.
—————— of men, iv. viii. 128—176.
Legislators, 173, 174.
Letter to Mrs. Wheeler, v.
Libertinism, 85.
Liberty, 196, 211.
Life, domestic, 203, 212.
Logic, 29.
Lyons, 204.

M.

Machinery, 183.
Machines, 89, 192.
Magic, 3, 194.
Majority 7.
Man, 93, 196. (See Men.)
Marriage, x. xiii. 40, 41, 55, 62, 63, 64, 67, 98, 104, 167, 171.
Masters, 210, 213.
Meats, 197.
Melancholy, 212.
Men, 12, 15, 16, 19, 22, 26, 32, 54, 118, 125, 167, 171, 191, 208, 210.
Mill, Mr., viii. 3, 4, 8, 9, 10, 11, 12, 13, 14, 25, 26, 27, 28, 29, 30, 40, 42, 44, 89, 159, 185.
Mind, enlargement of, 67, 122, 164, 190, 213.

Misery, 213.
Modesty, 192, 204.
Moiety, 171.
Mole, xiii.
Monopoly, 173, 206.
Morality, 35, 91, 167, 192, 213.
Morals, v. xii.
Morning, 209, 212.
Mothers, 42, 210.
Motives, 202.
Moving-spring, 203.
Mystification, 181.

N.

Nature, 16, 181, 199, 206, 211.
Negroes, 16, 69.
Nurse, 141.

O.

Obedience, 63, 67, 74, 78, 88, 192, 209.
Occasions, 91.
Offices, 174.
Oligarchy, 145.
Opinion, 35, 43, 45, 53, 61, 69, 159, 160.
Oppression, 96, 202, 206, 211.
Organization, vii. 38, 60, 62, 93, 95, 97, 151, 155, 171, 172, 177, 205.
Owen, Mr., 204.
Ox, 49.

P.

Pains, 205.
Paragraphs of "Article" respecting women, *title-page*, vii. 9.
Parallel of male and female legislation, 127, 145.
Parents, 212.
Part I. 3—20.
—— II. 21, 213.
Partners, 94.
Partnership, of injustice, 130.
Patience, 140.
Patronage, vi.
Peculiarities, 204.

INDEX.

Permission, 90.
Persecution, 201.
Perseverance, 140.
Persuasion, 17, 132, 176.
Petition, 210.
Philosophers, 7, 86, 171, 195.
Philosophy, 12, 16, 82.
Pleasure, 54, 74, 76, 77, 79, 80, 82, 101, 210.
Poison, 91.
Political economy, xiv. 42.
Politicians, 171.
Possession, joint, ix.
Postures, 191.
Power, vi. 7, 13, 16, 91, 185.
Prejudice, 183.
Preuves, judiciaires, 3.
Pride, 192.
Principle. (See Law.)
Prison discipline, 3.
Privations, 35, 205.
Probity, or moral aptitude, 40, 60, 128, 135.
Professions, 169
Professors, 172.
Project, 138.
Property, 39, 57, 87, 88, 173, 192, 200.
Proscription, 20, 31, 37.
Prosperity, 48.
Prostitute, 126, 212.
Prostitution, 200, 202.
Prostration, 17.
Protection, 27, 32, 63, 87, 88, 103, 167, 211, 212.
Prudence, 191.
Punishments, 35, 78, 159, 167, 197, 206.
Puppets, 212.

Q.

Qualities, 128, 129, 188, 193.
Question 1st of Part II. 25.
———— 2nd of do. 114.
———— 3rd of do. 155.
Question, general, of women, 186.

R.

Race, human, xiv. 171, 205, 208, 211.
Reciprocity, 172. 199
Reformers, xiv.
Remedy, 199.
Remonstrance, 194.
Remuneration, 197.
Repeal, 162.
Representation, 31, 36, 145, 177.
———————— virtual, 27, 58, 144.
Representatives, 144, 145, 175.
Reproach, 201.
Republican, 196.
Restraints, 43, 88, 101, 151, 159, 207.
Rewards, natural, 206.
Ridicule, 143, 144.
Rights, civil, 26, 59, 114, 172.
———— political, 1, 19, 25, 28, 30, 33, 107, 108, 114, 121, 148, 155, 165, 169, 174, 177, 180, 182, 209.
Rivalship, 196.
Roland, Madame, 194.
Rose, xii.

S.

Sanction, 128.
Sarcasm, 143.
Sauces, 189.
Schools, public, 209.
Science, 183.
Scorn, 68.
Scotland, 204.
Secresy, 172, 203.
Security, 8, 166.
Self-control, 44, 73, 192.
Self-government, 47, 59, 67, 89.
Selfishness, 15, 56, 124.
Senses, pleasures of, xii. 76, 210.
Sensualist, 64.

INDEX.

Sensuality, 77.
Sex, 178, 209, 212.
—— neutral, 179, 196.
Similarity, 38, 40.
Single women, 27.
Shame, 73, 103.
Sheep, 103.
Situation of women at large, 113, 177, 186, 212.
Slave-codes, 56.
Slavery, x. 69, 103, 170.
Slaves, x. 6, 7, 32, 42, 49, 64, 67, 70, 126, 164, 187, 195, 196, 203.
Slumber, 210.
Social improvement, xiv. 151.
—— science, xiv.
Society, new state of, ix. 155, 183.
Solitude, 212.
Sons, 37, 39, 49, 53.
Sounds, 191.
Stages of human improvement, 151.
Strength, 17, 120, 128, 133, 156, 189, 190, 211.
Stupidity, 179.
Submission, 68, 194.
Summary of argument respecting adult daughters, 53.
———— wives, 108.
———— of Question 2, Part II. 150.
———— of Question 3, do. 182.
Superiority, 204.
Superstition, 63, 79, 81, 185, 193, 213.
Sympathy, 14, 34, 49, 94, 96, 122, 132, 143, 149, 212.
System, sexual, of morals, 193, 194.

T.

Tactiques des Assemblées Legislatives, viii. 3.

Talents, 199, 206.
Temperance, 193.
Tendency, 177, 180, 181, 184.
Terrors, superstitious, 81.
Thaises, 213.
Theme, vi.
Theorie des Peines et des Recompenses, 3.
Theory, 116.
Three fourths, 11, 15.
Thriftiness, 193.
Title to happiness, 120.
Tools, 193.
Topics of letter to Mrs. Wheeler, iii.
—— of Part I. 1.
—— of Part II. Question 1 : 21.
—— do. Question 2 : 114.
—— do. Question 3 : 152.
—— of Address to Women, 154.
Traités de Legislation, 3.
Trial by battle, 142.
Truth, vi. 137, 139, 208.
Tyrant, 86.

U.

Unfeminine, 193.
United States of North America, 105, 135.
Unmarried women. (See Single.)
Uses of political rights, 121.
Usurpations, 117.
Usury, 3.
Utility, viii. ix. xiv. 3, 4, 20, 86, 159, 165, 171, 184, 186, 195, 208.

V.

Vacuum of mind, 81.
Vanity, 190.
Vices, 142, 144.
Vicissitudes, 92.
Victims, 105, 212.
Violence, 88.
Voluntariness, 90, 142.
Voluntary associations. (See Association.)

INDEX.

Vote, 174.
Vow of obedience, 71, 209.

W.

Warrior, 141.
Wars, 142, 156, 183.
Wealth, should be distributed according to cheerful exercise of talents for common good, x. 48, 203.
West India slavery. (See Slavery.)
West Indies, 6, 16, 105.
Wheeler, Mrs.: Frontispiece, v.
Widows, 30.
Will, 203.
Wisdom, vii. 195.
Wishes, 175.
Wives, third division of women, 27, 54.
—— *compelled* to submit to inequalities of marriage-code, absurdly called a contract, 55.
—— deprived of self-government, 58.
—— liable to assaults and imprisonment, 59.
—— dependent on husbands for sexual enjoyments—husbands not on them, 60.
—— marriage-code renders wives *slaves*, 65.
—— evils of slavery as pernicious to women as to men, 68.
—— marriage vow of obedience a superfluous insult, 71.
—— slavery of wives not justifiable for happiness of husbands, 73.
—— obedience to fathers is transferred to husbands, 74.
—— equal pleasures of senses are deemed *immoral* in wives, 77.
Wives, restraints and punishments of husbands and wives unequal, 78.
—— from social pleasures imprisonment debars wives, 79.
—— from intellectual, want of education and power of imprisonment, 80.
—— female West India slaves are not so controlled, 83—87.
—— are deprived of exercise of volition, thence of morality, 89.
—— are liable to tremendous vicissitudes in life, 93.
—— sympathy is lessened by difference of organization, 94.
—— difference of organization is even used as a justification of oppression, 96, 192.
Wolf, 104.
Women, living in their fathers' establishments, 9, 14, 18, 21.
—— without fathers or husbands, 27.
—— disadvantages in their competition with men, 32.
—— viii. 14, 15, 16, 54, 56, 57, 62, 63, 64, 66, 70, 74, 77, 80, 83, 93, 94, 97, 99, 100, 107, 108, 112, 113, 116, 118, 119, 130, 160, 172, 187, 198, 208, 211.
Wolstonecroft, Mary, vii.
Wrongs, 210.

Y.

Youth, 200, 209, 212.

ERRATA AND ADDENDA.

Page 1, line 6, for *human* read *political* rights.

Page 45, line 28. To this place transfer from pages 51 and 52 the paragraph respecting contrariety of interest, beginning with " The father," and ending with " individual happiness."

Page 88, line 2. After the words " Protection indeed !" add, "Of security of person or personal protection she is by the law expressly deprived. To all the ordinary *assaults* of her husband, to the compulsion and restraints of her husband on her actions and powers of locomotion, she is delivered up.—Of property and the ordinary means of acquiring it, she is deprived ; of security of person she is unblushingly deprived also.—The law affords her protection ! —She is out of the pale of the law.—*The law excludes her from protection* against the vices and violences of her husband ; from that equal protection which one man enjoys against another man. —Instead of *greater* protection, which justice would give her in consequence of her physical weakness and the domestic facilities of oppression, the law gives her less protection, gives her none except against extreme abuses."